THE

WORLD'S BOOK;

OR,

KEY TO SPIRITUAL LIFE.

THOUGHTS AND SUGGESTIONS

ON

SPIRITUAL MANIFESTATIONS,

OR

EXTRACTS FROM THE PRIVATE JOURNAL

OF

AN AMERICAN LADY,

BASING THE SPIRITUAL DEVELOPMENTS OF THE DAY UPON SCRIPTURE AND THE FIXED LAWS OF NATURE AND MIND.

CLEVELAND, O.:
KING AND COMPANY.

1855.

CONTENTS.

CHAPTER VI.

CHAPTER VII.

CHAPTER VIII.

PART SECOND.

LAWS OF THE SPIRITUAL MANIFESTATION.

CHAPTER IX.

CHAPTER X.

CHAPTER XI.

CHAPTER XII.

CHAPTER XIII.

CHAPTER XIV.

CHAPTER XV.

CHAPTER XVI.

Chapter XVII.

Chapter XVIII.

Chapter XIX.

Chapter XX.

Chapter XXI.

APPENDIX.

DEDICATION.

"THEN Agrippa said unto Paul, Thou art permitted to speak for thyself. Then Paul stretched forth his hand and answered for himself.

"I think myself happy, king Agrippa, because I shall answer for myself this day before thee, touching all the things whereof I am accused.

"Especially, because I know thee to be expert in all customs and questions which are among the Jews: wherefore I beseech thee to hear me patiently."—*Bible.*

The undersigned begs leave to dedicate this Book to the President of this American Republic, as a tribute of respect to the highest executive of her beloved country, from considerations of gratitude due her country, when contrasting with other governments its blessings, under whose broad, Eagle-spread pinions of liberty the advocates of truth find shelter from the hawk-talons of bigotry and oppression, from inquisition and death,

Confident from his reputed intelligence and great moral worth, he will not disdain to investigate any subject, popular or unpopular, moral or spiritual, that can lay claim to truth, and to the advancement and well being of the people (or of a private individual even) of this great commonwealth.

With assurances of high regard,

AN AMERICAN LADY.

INTRODUCTORY REMARKS.

THE object of this book is to throw light upon the spiritual manifestations of the day, and aid the honest inquirers after spiritual knowledge, by giving them the key which unlocks the mystery of the power of evil over the human mind, and opens wide the door to spiritual life, to those who will enter to explore this mine of truth, and are willing to labor to separate the dross from the gold, for the sake of the gold; the wheat from the chaff for the sake of the wheat; thereby to separate the evil from the good by obeying the law of spiritual life. The two are combined when taken in their natural state, in the human soul, as well as in the field or mine.

The writer feels great embarrassment in giving that part of the manuscript illustrating the law controlling the manifestation which refers to her private life. The nature of the instruction is so adapted to, and blended with the personal *inquiry* and circumstances, more or less through all these writings, that she knows not how to separate the two, and do justice to the subject.

She attempted to suppress those chapters entirely upon angelic ministrations, and the greater part of the instruction to her how to become an instrument of good — a reliable writer under this influence, "A workman that needeth not to be ashamed." The separation seemed to mutilate the whole, for which she could bring no substitute. The object and design of the manifestion was defeated, when thus concealed, in its practical results to herself and others, as learners in the school of spiritual life. For the cause of truth she gives the whole without further apology. As far as her personal history is concerned, she must throw herself upon the clemency of the reader, and take shelter under the established tolerated custom of autobiographers.

The writer has never met in a "circle," so called, for the investigation of this subject, to profit by the experience of others, nor with but a few who wrote in this manner. Neither has she had the opportunity to read more than a few paragraphs written by those called "Mediums," but which she would term *pupils* in the school of spiritual life.

Her inquiries after truth have not been of man, nor from books, but at the footstool of Sovereign Mercy, who has promised to give wisdom to them that ask. To Him alone who created mind has she looked for the law controlling these developments, when her senses assured her the facts developed were not illusions or delusions in their effects upon the passive hand and teachable mind, but were traceable to unseen yet real causes, though unseen and spiritual. She looked from the effect to the cause to learn the law producing the effect.

Consequently in her expectation and Ignorance of the way, she was led on step by step, from the reply given to one inquiry, to make others, without any premeditated system (which has occurred to her since she might have done, and thereby made these extracts more acceptable to others), until the law controlling the manifestation was made manifest, by tracing effect to cause, and cause to effect, which divested the subject of much of the mysterious and miraculous appearance it at first assumed and planted it upon a common sense, practical, Biblical basis, a firm rock where truth might stand and be stripped of its false covering, which both its advocates and opposers had clothed it with, and the world be benefitted by its developments.

The above paragraph accounts for the abrupt introduction of subjects, as well as the frequent repetition of the same sentiment. It is attributable to her abrupt inquiries and slowness to comprehend things written, doubts and cavilings, which not only interrupted the flow of thought, but oft obscured its sense. This the writer regrets, and did at the time. Her natural importunate desire (which, by the by, had to be crucified) to know all the whys and wherefores, before she acted or believed, has often marred the connection and clearness of the subjects.

It is impossible for her now to amend this defect in these pages, or to change the peculiar style and brevity of stating facts, "Teaching like one having authority." The defects in the style and diction are apparent to the writer, and have caused her much perplexity of thought why the style and diction were not as perfect and pure as the truth and the source from which it emanates, until she settled the point. Her uncultivated powers were, in a way unknown to herself, the cause of this defect, and would yet be accounted for philosophically when the hidden law of mind was better understood. The mind while engaged in this operation of receiving communications, apparently makes no more effort in composing and in originating ideas, than one does when he listens with such fixed attention to another, as to forget himself in the new and important thoughts suggested by the speaker. And surely the listener could not claim to originate the ideas because adapted to his comprehension. And the attempt to compose or originate sentences after this sort, without premeditation or purpose, soon convinced the writer that such random thoughts of the intellect would distract and bewilder the mind, instead of quieting, instructing and leading it on as the child is led, step by step into new regions of thought and to new scenes of contemplation, without any further effort than to follow and walk with the guiding hand.

She is also aware that this volume is but the stripling David when compared to other published works, or the Goliaths of talent, that have taken the field, both for and against this disputed subject. Yet she solicits a place in the background as a silent observer to send forth these thoughts and suggestions as given to her, clad with its own plain, unadorned, matter-of-fact garb, and if called out to battle with the defiers of its faith, she fears not but its well-balanced zeal may be able to war a good warfare, and bear off at last the standard arms of its opposers, as trophies of its victory, into the audience chamber of the King of kings, who she trusts sent it forth, since truth is "mighty in pulling down strongholds."

That the true key of knowledge has been given which unlocks the door to the hidden law of mind, as well as to the mysterious manifestations now before the world, and will bring to light eventually from this mine, important concealed treasures hitherto unknown, she has not a shadow of a doubt. To her vision the hidden laws of the human mind are beginning to be unfolded, that we may know more of the law of spiritual life, in what its safety and dangers consist, its blessings and its penalties. Vast as are the capacities and capabilities of the human soul, the same fixed and unbending law that develops the affectional powers of the infant mind, and fixes its destiny, controls also and holds accountable the highest created intelligence in the universe of worlds. All are subjects of the same spiritual law, and bear the impress of the great first Cause, who is the model law and architect of mind, the originator of spiritual life. This key has served the purpose in part for which it was given to her mind, consequently she considers it belongs no longer exclusively to herself, nor to the spiritual developments of the age, but to every being clothed with mind.

Should this book effect the object designed, that is, to throw light upon the subject treated, and aid the honest inquirer after spiritual truth so to die to self as to be delivered from this body of death, and seek to be risen with Christ in newness of life, she would have occasion to rejoice with exceeding great joy that this cup was ever put to her lips, to drink alone amid the jeers and contempt, censure and condemnation of many.

NOTE EXPLANATORY OF DRAWING FIRST.

In March, 1852, when the writer was caviling as to whether this manifestation was really the influence of another mind upon her own, or whether it was the unknown operations of her own mind acting upon things once known and forgotten and now developed in this manner, she was directed to make such figures or lines as the hand was influenced to make, independent of the knowledge of the mind, to give her such additional proof that it was not some secret and hidden operation of her mind or memory, but that the instruction given was designed to illustrate important spiritual truth in agreement with the Word of God.

She commenced, as before, by placing the pencil in the center of the drawing-sheet, when in perhaps an hour's time, in the presence of a friend, the opposite sketch was given. When completed, she was wholly at a loss to know what it meant. Her husband coming in at the time, asked for an explanation, which she could not give until it was explained by the writing which accompanies the drawing.

In December last, when she was directed to copy the drawing for this volume on a smaller scale — not having written for a long time with the influence upon the hand — she took the original copy and placed it before her, with a measuring rule to get as exact a copy as possible in a smaller compass. After spending some little time in the effort without success, it was suggested, Why not trust the same influence to draw it as at first? as she found it so difficult to draw it by measuring with the rule. She at once placed the hand passively on the paper, and with a degree of surprise (after all that she had witnessed of this mysterious unseen power), to find such readiness and exactness to execute with the passive hand, what she with the helps referred to had failed to do. Parts of it were drawn with the eyes closed, especially the outer sweeping circles, which reassured herself the agency was not the illusion of her own mind. The whole was drawn the same as before, with a little addition, *viz.*, the lines representing the love of self, the lust of the flesh, and the pride of life. The written explanations were given then as before in the original sketch.

The writer has no apology to make for stating simply and truthfully these mysterious operations. Facts are stubborn things. Skepticism, derision, or unbelief, can not annihilate truth. "Though it fall, it shall rise again."

PART FIRST.

AUTOBIOGRAPHICAL.

CHAPTER I.

THOUGHTS AND SUGGESTIONS ON SPIRITUAL MANIFESTATIONS.

THE writer, at the beginning of her experience, as portrayed in this volume, seemed to herself to be led "in a way she had not known," and she was therefore exceedingly anxious to understand the nature of that experience. As she had been brought into this way without seeking it, according to her belief, by patiently and confidingly waiting upon the Lord, she expected direction, so she now sought unto that same source of light and truth for knowledge upon this point; and the first eight chapters of the work, which constitute the *first part*, are mainly autobiographical, the matter being taken from that portion of her journal which records her inquiries and the answers given, respecting the origin, character, and general scope of this mode of receiving truth and light from God.

April, 1852.—I. *Ques.* How is the hand influenced to write, by what power, while the brain is unconscious of what is to be written, or sketched?

Ans. Through the motive power of spirit upon the nervous system.

Ques. What is meant by motive power of spirit?

Ans. The force of organic life.

Ques. Well, what is organic life?

Ans. It is the connecting link between spirit and matter, and the channel of spiritual operation between the body and spirit, as well as between spirit and spirit.

Ques. Is this manifestation, then, supernatural, as many suppose?

Ans. It is supernatural, or above the laws of nature which govern the physical universe; but not above the natural laws which control spiritual life.

God governs the worlds of creation, as well as man the work of his hands, by fixed laws. These laws are natural, because adapted to the organization of each; yet spirit is above matter, as God is above his works.

There is a law governing mind as well as matter.

This spiritual law emanates from the concentrated excellencies of the Divine moral nature, necessarily subjecting every created intelligence in the wide universe of God, whether angels or men, to its obedience or penalty.

This divine law is based upon the moral integrity of God, therefore is unchangeable; governing with the same unbending power, as when men and angels were sinless. No other code could possibly have been transmitted from the concrete perfections of the Divine nature to man created in his image.

Ques. What is the design of God in this manifestation to the world?

Ans. To teach men the affinity existing between the spiritual and material worlds. The law of spiritual attraction, of both good and evil, existing between minds in the body and spirits invisible to man, is one important feature in the spiritual developments of the present day.

To show more tangibly that man's choice of good and evil fixes his destiny, and the power of his volition and faith to resist and break every snare of evil, independent of his fallen nature and surrounding circumstances.

This manifestation is designed to show the world of mankind what they are; in how many ways they are in league with Satan, he operating by them, and in them through the spirit of selfishness. And what the world may become by faith and holiness, if they will obey the spiritual law of life.

These tangible demonstrations, in one form or other of the presence of unseen spiritual agencies of both good and evil, will be made to the whole world, each proving their source by the nature of the communication received. What is from God harmonizes with the doctrines of his Word. The new truths brought to light by the teachings of the Holy Spirit, and based upon the Word of his law and faith, is the engrafted Word which is able to save the soul, because grafted into the old stock, which bears the same fruit with the branch. "The Spirit and the Word agree."

Ques. Can all persons write under this influence of the motive power of spirit?

Ans. Yes. But the spirit of self which is the only inherent depravity of the human soul, will greatly mar the work, by attracting evil influences from the spirit world, like itself. When self is slain, this gift or power which belongs to the law of spiritual life, may become a channel of great good to the soul. If self is not crucified and the soul purified from all sin, like all other perverted gifts, it becomes to him a source of evil, he can reap no profit from it. The corrupt fountains will send forth their bitter waters.

Ques. If the soul desires to be rightly led, will not that good desire protect him from evil influences?

Ans. No. Good desires cannot save the soul from the power of evil; it must, from choice, part with all evil, and resist it continually. Faith and purity are the channels of truth; self and sin of error.

Ques. How is it with the writings of those who have received justifying grace, yet are not saved to the uttermost from all sin.

Ans. Each individual will find his spiritual state portrayed by the nature of the writings he gets, taking the Word for his standard. The evil heart of unbelief in God's Word, will get corresponding doctrines: Thou shalt not surely die, the primeval doctrine of the source of self and sin. The believer not wholly sanctified will get writings true and false, because his state is a mixed one. The selfish, carnal mind attracts evil and repels good.

When faith and holiness predominate, and possess the soul entire, good is attracted and truth is communicated. Then this manifestation becomes a channel of intercourse between man and angels and God, leading him in ways of pleasantness and paths of peace.

When the dynamic power of spiritual communications is better understood, it will show the combined wisdom and goodness of God towards the world he died to redeem. Then the chaff will be separated from the wheat, error from truth, light from darkness.

Ques. How are the powers of the mind used in the writings?

Ans. The mind does not dictate, yet the powers of the mind are used as the channel or medium for the higher spiritual force or power to work through when prepared.

Ques. Will this be illustrated to my mind?

Ans. Your powers of body and mind are the machine. The motive power of spiritual influence puts the machine in motion.

Ques. Why, then, if the mind is like a machine, is a preparation necessary?

Ans. The machinery for fabrics, differs from the machinery for telescopic discovery.

Ques. Will this be explained, how this can be applied to the mind of a medium?

Ans. The one illustrates the selfish heart as a channel, the other that heart purified and prepared to view things above, in the heavens, through the agency of the Holy Spirit.

The reliable writer must be holy; the heart must be cleansed from all the dross of self. Christ, the fountain of life, must abide by living faith in the soul, inspiring all the thoughts, controlling the will. This state attracts all good influences and repels evil, and enables the writer to resist not only his own foes, but the evil influences which would act upon the passive writer,—which the minds of others attract who seek direction or spiritual instruction through this channel from curious or selfish motives. Strive to become a workman that needeth not to be ashamed.

Ques. Is my heart still selfish?

Ans. Yes. In some things you have a will; if that will is crossed, you feel grieved; self is disappointed.

Ques. Can I ever rise superior to this feeling in this world?

Ans. Yes; lie as clay in the hands of the potter; be as willing to be brought low as exalted, if that most promotes the cause of truth. The spirit of self must die before you can write reliably for others. Fixed laws govern this manifestation. Keep this in mind, give up the past, let it all go, and obey the laws of spiritual life — all will be well.

Ques. I wish to inquire more about this force or motive power, which moves the hand to write. What causes the painful sensation in the arm, as soon as I think of writing?

Ans. The effect of force upon the nervous system sufficient to control the hand, mingling with the nervous fluid of the system; because volition is suspended, a power sufficient or equal to volition must be employed to control the hand. This foreign force or power gives a painful sensation to the peculiarly sensitive nerves, especially if the nerves are suffering from physical causes.

Ques. How is this foreign influence subject to the will, or in other words, how is it, that the hand is influenced whenever the person wishes to write?

Ans. The influence is ever present with you, and readily obeys your slightest wish.

Ques. Is this influence spontaneous in the natural world, or does it come to man through special agencies appointed of God?

Ans. It is the connecting link between matter and

spirit, as well as between spirit and spirit. Knowledge is transmitted from the wise to the unwise in spiritual things as in earthly. Earth is the shadow of heaven in many things.

Ques. Does not God directly dwell in the holy soul, and direct the mind, independent of angelic or other agencies?

Ans. Christ is the true bread of life to every believing soul. This life of Christ in the soul attracts all holy influences to itself, and brings the recipient of God's grace into fellowship with the saints of light.

Ques. How is it that evil influences, as well as good, control the hand, if this manifestation is from God?

Ans. Evil is subversive of good. Man's evil, immoral state, naturally attracts evil influences to itself. The affinity, when once formed, is stronger than the human will. Therefore Paul said, "when I would do good, evil is present with me." Nothing but Almighty power can deliver the soul from this evil, after the mind has willingly yielded to sin and thereby attracted evil. Self is Satan's stronghold. Resist the devil; pray, deliver me from evil, as Jesus taught.

Ques. If these manifestations are from God, why is Satan permitted to take the lead in their developments?

Ans. There is more evil than good in the world to impress the mind with the truth of evil influences unseen, acting in unison with the evil indulged in by man; necessarily this must be made manifest by wicked men, according to the Word of God. A pure fountain can not send forth bitter water.

The good physician seemingly aggravates disease by using means to develop what is intricate, before he can apply the remedy or convince the patient he is so diseased. So in this, man must see and realize his danger, before he will cry, deliver me from evil. Evil never works a cure, but feels the need of a remedy. Say not let us do evil that good may come. The true light makes darkness more manifest.

The manifestation of evil is not so much to point the way to heaven, as to expose the concealed road to hell. The Bible teaches the way of the Lord perfectly, in redeeming souls, yet obscurely in his permissive providence, while these manifestations more fully develop the ways of evil, which bring suffering to man, that man may forsake self and sin, and trust in God.

When this truth fastens upon the mind, that the permissive providences of God, which appear so mysterious to man, are only the will of God developed in protecting the moral agency of beings whom he made in his own image, and that he holds them responsible in consequence of this, for their acts—not that God approves or sanctions evil, but protects man's free-agency as a moral being—when this conviction is deeply inwrought in the soul, that God wills not what he permits; that this permission is the necessary result of free agency, it will bring to its aid Bible truth on the offices of the Holy Spirit to help man's infirmities. The truth of God will take deeper root in honest hearts. Then the Spirit, which is the promised teacher and comforter of the people of God, will lead the soul into all truth, and show them things to come. "Then shall Zion arise and put on her beautiful garments of salvation; her light shall break forth as brightness, her salvation as a lamp that burneth."

Ques. What reply shall be made to individuals when

they say, there is no necessity for, or good to be derived from, these additional manifestations, as we already have the Word of God and the Holy Spirit to lead the church?

Ans. Has not God, in every age of the world, suited the developments of his will to men according to their ability to receive and obey? Ask why the giving of the law by Moses preceded the giving of the Gospel by Christ and the Apostles; then you will have the reason why the fullness of the Gospel dispensation should succeed the beginning of the revelation of the Gospel to man, which was good news, and glad tidings of great joy.

Ques. Will the writings of those instigated by Satan, be received by the world?

Ans. There is, in the natural heart, a reservoir for evil; unchecked by the spirit of love and truth, it would subvert and corrupt many minds from the simplicity of a life of faith in Christ.

Ques. Will my writing have that tendency?

Ans. Truth and error produce opposite effects. Truth cleanses the reservoir of the carnal mind, and makes it the well-spring of life, teaching the lips knowledge.

Ques. Is it my duty, or will it be required of me to write reprovingly again to others under this influence? I wish my faults corrected, yet I shrink from reproving others.

Ans. Your first inquiry should be, how can my powers and faculties of soul and body be best made a channel of spiritual good to others, rather than to please self and friends.

Ques. My reply would be, let me serve God. *Ans.*—Then follow, follow Jesus whithersoever he goeth. He was crucified between thieves. You know the voice of the Shepherd — listen. His voice is the still, small voice of love, lowliness, meekness, patience, forbearance. The voice proclaiming, love not the world, neither the things of the world. He that honoreth me, him will I honor. Listen to the voice of the good shepherd. Seek from him, in silent communings, your duty. The Spirit teacheth the way to everlasting life. The promise is sure to such as believe and obey.

Ques. Should one continue to write, unless all that is written is reliable?

Ans. Cease from self and error, give place to truth. The reliable workman must be holy.

Ques. How can I become so?

Ans. The Holy Spirit sanctifies.

Ques. What do I need to bring me into that state?

Ans. The full baptism of the Holy Ghost.

Ques. In what does this baptism consist?

Ans. The entire death of the carnal mind. The descent of the Spirit, filling the soul's capacity with the love of God.

Ques. Why will the Lord not give me that baptism now? I earnestly desire it.

Ans. You desire it, yet you shrink from the baptismal flame of suffering. You want this and that friend to lean upon. Naked and alone you must stand the refining flame. Who can abide the day of his coming? He is like the refiner's fire and the fuller's soap, and cleanses from all idolatry and household gods.

Ques. What more can I do than I have done?

Ans. Follow the leadings of the Spirit in this manifestation. Die the martyr's death.

Ques. Do I still love self more than God?

Ans. No. But you desire to take your friends and good name along with you, in serving God.

Ques. Is that wrong, to desire to be justly appreciated?

Ans. Seek not the honor that comes from man; but with a single eye trust in God for all you need, in time and eternity. The day of thy life is far spent. That thou doest, do quickly.

The crown is for the victor. The path of duty is the path of safety. So fight that you may obtain.

May 20, 1852.—II. *Ques.* I ask in deep affliction, Is there any instruction for me this morning?

Ans. Yes. The sayings of others must not trouble you; leave it all to God. Trust in God to lead the mind, as well as to heal the body. He will do both.

Ques. What shall I say to those who call this delusion, and the work of Satan, and sinful for a Christian to follow?

Ans. Remember what Christ said to Peter. What God has sanctified and cleansed, call not thou common or unclean.

Reason forbids the conclusion that the Lord has left his children to be deceived, or led by Satan, the enemy of God and man, when they seek to be led by God. The only way that Satan can be overcome, is by faith and prayer; through the power of the Holy Sanctifier, Son of God, Redeemer of the world.

Bring all your offerings to God; he will receive them, and give you himself in return. Soon you will be prepared to write in all safety for the good of the world. The Lord will make your enemies to be at peace with you. You will triumph in God, the rock of your salvation.

God turns and overturns Satan's devices, and delivers his people. When the wicked least expect it, their plans are overthrown.

June, 1852.— III. *Ques.* Am I required to write for my own benefit solely?

Ans. Some have been benefited already. When you are prepared, more will be.

Ques. What preparation is now necessary?

Ans. The baptismal flame must consume all dross.

Ques. Can I do any thing to hasten the work?

Ans. Patiently endure every thing that comes. The time is short before your deliverance will be wrought.

Ques. Am I now bearing all in a right spirit?

Ans. When you do, your sorrows will end. Learn this is the law of life in God, given to man. Then the soul will be risen with Christ — your days of mourning will be ended.

June, 1852. — IV. *Ques.* Is there any thing for ——?

Ans. No. He must not expect through this source further direction. He secretly rejects this influence as from God, when his wishes and selfish desires are crossed. So let him act upon his own judgment, which he regards as more safe than to be led by the Spirit of Truth, speaking to his heart. The belief of the overruling hand of God in his changes, would greatly relieve his anxious mind. Now he can not forecast, with any certainty, temporal or spiritual matters. God feeds the sparrow; especially the righteous, who trust in him, will he lead in the right way.

The safety of man depends upon his obedience to accompany his reliance on God to lead him. The trust of working or believing faith is the soul's rest. Faith is the power that prevails. Trust is the anchor of hope, which holds the vessel to its fastenings, on the Rock Christ Jesus. Faith brings the blessing, trust retains it.

July, 1852.—V. *Ques.* Dear Lord and Saviour, wilt thou teach me this morning, through this manifestation of the Spirit, the way more clearly?

Ans. Though I hide my face for a little moment, yet, in everlasting kindness will I gather you.

Ques. Are the views I expressed to —— correct, upon this subject?

Ans. Partly true, and partly not.

Ques. What is true?

Ans. The necessity of the medium being holy. The dynamic force of spiritual manifestations is not yet understood. The laws of attraction in nature, are emblematic of spiritual affinities, and are true in matter and spirit, as human experience can testify. Yet the great power of spiritual attraction, whether good or evil, over the passive hand and will, is a mystery the world is slow to receive, and the law remains yet to be disclosed. Be careful of theories; let facts demonstrate truths.

Ques. Will the Lord keep me from error, and guide me in this mysterious work?

Ans. In due time, you shall write in the knowledge of the heavenly, the things pertaining to godliness.

Ques. Who will teach me?

Ans. The Spirit of truth. He that winneth souls is wise. Work for God.

Ques. May I be taught things concerning my own state?

Ans. Yes.

Ques. Is my heart now separated from creature idols?

Ans. The buyers and sellers are cast out. But watch, Satan seeks to devour.

Ques. When shall I write?

Ans. Write when the mind is drawn to the work in sweetness of spirit, without anxiety.

Ques. Will Satan have power to draw me to write when I should not?

Ans. The evil influences, when evil spirits tempt you to write, come only when unbelief, or something wrong is indulged in the heart. Then resist. "Prove your own selves."

Ques. Do I draw evil influences, when I think wrong or uncharitably upon any subject?

Ans. Yes. All unbelief against God's Word and promise to guide, forgive, protect, deliver, and save, is sin. To despond is sin; to think uncharitably of God is sin. Walk by faith as did Abraham. When instruction into the future is given, of duty, as it was to Abraham, believe and obey as he did, nothing doubting.

Ques. Are Christians now taught as he was by God, both spiritual and temporal things?

Ans. Yes. When God sees best for the good of souls. Man's probationary life is a state of faith. Man is capable of great improvement in his mental and spiritual powers in the walk of faith. Each power and faculty should be a channel for spiritual communication from God to his soul; also a channel of good to others for Christ's sake.

God may speak to the soul direct by his Spirit, or by the instrumentality of angels and men, through the channels of the senses. Let the soul leave the manner to God to direct.

Have faith in God; trust him to lead and guide the

soul. He will separate the evil from the good, as the husbandman separates the chaff from the wheat.

Faith is godlike in its nature. This gift God gave man. It is an element inherent in the nature of the Supreme Being; uncreated therefore, undying in its nature, unlimited in its power, it cancels sin, sustains in sufferings, removes mountains of difficulties, moves the hand of God to open the storehouse of his treasures to his children's necessities; it makes manifest the secrets of God.

Faith in God is the vital breath of love. You can not love God without faith in him as your Creator and Redeemer. You can not love man, without faith in his truth. It is upon the same principle or law of mind man is required to love God, that he loves his friend.

Faith is the substance which dispels the shadow of uncertainty, by bringing God into the soul of all his promises.

The precious promises are soulless to unbelief, and mere mockeries of man's helpless condition. Faith brings God into his promises; then man lives not by bread alone, but by every word of God. God speaks in the works of creation to man; he speaks in his providences, as well as his written Word. The pure in heart see God in all his works and ways to the children of men. There is a deep, significant meaning in these words of the Lord: "Shall I do this thing, and not show it to my servant Abraham?" which you will comprehend, in proportion as you understandingly obey the voice of truth.

Ques. If the powers of my mind are used, why can I not command the words in which instruction is given, as though it were my own, when I attempt to repeat it to others?

Ans. It is the truth which is to be written upon the heart. The letter killeth and cumbers the mind, while the Spirit gives life and lets the soul go free.

This fulfills the promise made through the prophets and apostles:

"I will make a new covenant with my people after those days. I will put my law in their inward parts, and write it in their hearts. And I will be to them God, and they shall be to me a people."

"Then one shall not say to another, know ye the Lord, for all shall know me, from the least to the greatest."

The old covenant of works is ready to vanish away, while the new covenant written in the heart, in the inner man, is renewed day by day.

"When the Spirit of Truth is come, he will lead you into all truth, and show you things to come." "But ye have an unction from the Holy One, and knoweth all things."

"I have not written unto you because ye know not the truth, and that no lie is of the truth." Said the Spirit of Inspiration, "Who is a liar, but he that denieth that Jesus is the Christ. He is antichrist that denieth the Father and the Son."

"But the anointing which ye have received of him, abideth in you, and ye need not that any man teach you; but as the same anointing, teacheth you of all things, and is truth, and is no lie, and even as it hath taught you, ye shall abide in him."

Aug, 1852.—VI. *Ques.* My friend says the writings savor of my own style. The expressions are commonplace, and not beyond any ordinary capacity to dictate.

Ans. Those forms of expression are chosen by the Great Teacher, from your storehouse of knowledge, which will most readily convey truth to your mind. Such expressions are used as all minds are familiar with. Christ, in his teachings, took from every-day life, subjects with which the people were familiar, and used their own laws and customs and criticisms to instruct their faith and reprove their unbelief. He came down to man's capacities, and assumed their form.

By symbol and parable he taught divine and spiritual truths. His simplicity gave offense, because he came not in the wisdom of man's words to set up his spiritual reign.

Tongues are nothing, for they shall cease; knowledge vanish away; prophesies shall fail. But faith, hope, love, charity, abideth.

But the greatest of these is charity. Charity is the box of truth, and truth is the gem you seek. Now henceforth, feel no more desire to have instruction clothed in language superior to what mortals can command, for this would not convince the skeptic. When Christ spake as never man spake, the people said of him, he hath a devil.

Aug., 1852.— VII. I tremble in view of the high stand and source these teachings assume. My Christian friends now call me presumptuous and wicked, for presuming to think the Lord will control the hand, instead of departed friends.

Ques. What can I say to make others believe it is our privilege to be taught of the Holy Spirit in this manner of the Spirit's operation, as well as in prayer and meditation?

Ans. This testimony of the Spirit will accompany what is written to all who will receive it. It shall be written upon their hearts, and in their minds. The diversity of the Spirit's operations are channels of wealth to the soul. Such shall know of the doctrine, such shall feel it is truth, and the truth shall make them free.

This is the victory truth shall gain over error, and by the word of their testimony. The truth shall prevail. Here is the work of the Spirit in writing his law upon the mind, instead of upon tables of stone, as the Spirit which was in the Prophets and Apostles did signify or teach. Christ is the bridegroom of the Church. For he hath said, I am married unto you; thy Maker is thy husband.

Look within for the kingdom. The kingdom of heaven is within you, as Jesus taught. If the kingdom is within, the King is there also; if the King, the royal treasures are in the kingdom, the robes of righteousness, the wedding garment, with which to clothe his guests. There the royal banquets are held in his own kingdom. There the feast of love, the triumphs of victory will be celebrated. Then Christ will be risen in all hearts, then will individuals learn what is the rest prepared for those that love God. The stone which was cut out of the mountain without hands, shall fill the whole earth, or the individual heart. These individual kingdoms compose the universal kingdom of the saints of the Most High, in the Jerusalem above, as individuals compose communities on earth.

He that overcometh shall have a white stone, and in the stone a new name, which none can read but he that receiveth it. This stone signifies Christ risen in the soul, which is to increase and fill the whole soul. The new name is the new covenant of love written in their hearts and minds, to signify they were the true sons of God who were led by the Spirit, in the midst of this unbelieving and perverse nation.

I will sprinkle clean water upon you, and ye shall be clean. I will cleanse you from all filthiness of the flesh and spirit, that is, the spirit of self in alliance with evil. I will put my law of love within you, and write it upon the table of your hearts. I will be your God, and ye shall be my people.

Resisting evil, cleaving unto righteousness by the adhesive power of love, as naturally as matter adheres to particles of matter, to which it is joined by the fixed laws of the universe. Yea, stronger, for force may separate bodies in matter united. But the soul risen with Christ, and abiding in him from consent or choice, neither principalities nor powers, things present or things to come; neither height nor depth nor any other creature can separate the soul from Christ.

Thus shall the varied manifestations of the Spirit prepare the way for Christ to enter the temple of the heart, as John prepared the way of Christ in the wilderness. Such as received John's testimony, were prepared to receive Christ's teachings.

Such as receive this truth of the Spirit's teachings, as it is their privilege and duty, and seek to be led by the Spirit of Truth, will find they seek not in vain.

"Let him that lacketh wisdom ask of God, who giveth to all men liberally and upbraideth not, and it shall be given him." He that closes his eye to facts, because enveloped in mystery, obeys not this injunction, to ask of God. He leans to his own understanding, instead of seeking wisdom from the Lord.

CHAPTER II.

ANGELIC INFLUENCE.

Sep., 1852.— I. Now let us retrospect the past, and we will show you how merciful and long-suffering have been the ways of the Lord towards you.

Again, recall thy renewed conversation made *Aug.* 10, 1849, after the decease of a loved one. Then thou didst say, all my affections I give to thee; my life, my health, my reputation, my ease, my all in all, for God and to God. The exchange was made. God gave you himself, and then gave you to the world to develop through you his good-will to man in the truth of angelic ministrations.

God took a part of thy consecrated affections, and in an hour of deep affliction, in the developments of his providence, gradually entwined them around the truth of angelic ministrations. When the desire and expectation of life was cut off by the rapid progress of disease, and you placed among strangers, without the assiduity and sympathy of anxious friends to draw your mind earthward; shut in from the world, the sick-room became to you the observatory of the secret workings of the human soul, and of the machinations of Satan in destroying man. Then the guardian care of angels also over man, broke in upon your mental vision like a glorious reality. You were then taught many precious truths, through the agency of angelic ministrations, never before conceived of by you as possible. Yet you doubted and feared at every turn, and often repelled holy influences from you, by fearing delusion. You feared to believe (lest you should be uncharitable) the disclosures made to you through angelic ministrations, of the secret sins of others, that you might do them good. How often you have grieved the Spirit by your unwillingness to bear this cross, to pluck souls as brands from the burning, who might have been startled from their dreamy state, by the exposure to them of their heart-sins, and idolatries.

The instruction given you, and the interest and sympathy manifested by them in temporal as well as spiritual things for the good of man, was also often questioned and rejected as well as partially received.

When you did act up to the light you had, and communicated to the individuals concerned the disclosures given, and heard their concession of its truth, afterward you suffered Satan to come in like a flood and destroy your peace through fearfulness and unbelief of its source, which prevented further developments of their delight to minister unseen to man.

How often have you been so convinced of this truth, you have said I will yield to these sweet influences and copy their example, and do the will of the Lord on earth, as fearlessly as angels do in heaven. Again when some cross was presented self did not love, you shrunk from duty, and if driven out by the Spirit, you obeyed so reluctantly, from necessity rather than choice, you lost your reward. While you would embrace the cross of ordinary duties with cheerfulness, yet you loved not to be known as being identified with these mental exercises, until their truth was verified to other minds. The cross was new and strange, and unlovely to the mixed state of mind, where the spirit of self is cherished. The Lord pitied your infirmities, and raised up such friends as he saw you needed to strengthen your faith and hold you on your way. Now because of the misapprehensions of the truth by some, and the rejection of it by others, you are praying to die to these manifestations, and to forget all future good promised, thinking you must now do so, to die to self, and escape delusion.

Here is your mistake. Self has had nothing to do with them, only to oppose them. The God of providence and angels, and the friends given you, have co-operated to prevent you from taking the work out of God's hands, and appropriating it again as before; according to former habits of thought, because the way was new to you, you feared at every step, error and delusion.

When the manifestation assumed the form of writing, your ignorance of the law controlling this form of the manifestation again overwhelmed you; sincere in the gift of your affections to God, it was the good pleasure of the Lord to so discipline your affections in this work, as to enable him to take possession of your gift.

This could not be, while self was in the affections, for self can remain where friends are turned out, when the flesh is overcome, when the world is given up. But where self is, Satan is not overcome, as Christ overcame the prince of darkness. Satan in self still tempts, worries, accuses you, and opposes Christ from taking possession of your gifts (*i. e.*), of your entire affections.

The soul, conscious of surrendering all as far as it knows to God, wonders at Christ's delay to accept and heal. None can be healed but such as will part with self too, for Christ must heal from the oppression of the Devil, whose spirit is in alliance with self, and is the last to be overcome, that the traveler may walk uniformly by faith with Christ in white. Satan shall not harm you, he may solicit, but can not tempt or force you into sin. "This is your victory, even your faith."

Now self must die; "Let the dead bury their dead." Let self in friends bury your dead body of self-love wherever they please, or cast it out, too vile for burial; you have nothing to do with it. "But follow thou me!" Jesus said to his disciples, still he says it to thee.

While you keep your gift upon the altar for sacrifice, in sincerity, you must obey the voice of the Spirit, for God is in the manifestation to you. God presented it to you. He called out your affections, your sympathies, and all circumstances. He laid them in the sick-room, and developed them as he saw fit without your knowledge or permission of the way you were to be led. He used them then, and has since, to his own glory, to reprove and save from sin.

Be content to be thus singularly led, a messenger for Christ on earth. Others will follow. "Who is so dumb as my messenger, and who so blind as my servant?". Both dumb and blind to the calls of self, worldly prudence, worldly policy, worldly ambition.

Delight to be active in the will of God on earth, as angels are in heaven. Could your selfish petitions have been granted, to have the past obliterated from mind and memory, and you excused from them in future, you would have failed to accomplish the work designed for you to do here, for the glory of God. Pure love is disinterested. Think of your Master, who not only was reviled by his enemies, but is very often disobeyed, neglected and forgotten, set aside for self and idols, by his followers. While self is in the heart, friends as well as enemies will reject these direct teachings, if it expose or reprove their selfish inclinations, as they have done in the past. Some will turn your enemy for telling them the truth. "The servant is not above his Lord." Christ said, "I have told you the truth, for which of these sayings do ye stone me?"

There was no self in Christ, yet he was a man of sorrow and suffering and agony, grief and death. And still he is crucified afresh, and put to open shame by the little love and little faith of his followers.

Ques. How can I continue to write, when the communications are so misrepresented as to result in my injury, although good to others? They have been misrepresented by some who solicited them, and are used by other individuals to destroy my reputation and consistency; and I am called presumptuous and led by Satan (by the good even), to the dishonor of the cause I love.

Ans. True, truth alone makes free. All did not receive the truth from the lips of Christ. The loss will not be yours. To you, dark has been the hour and still must be. Let the withholding of proper sympathy remind you of the hour when Jesus said, "Could ye not watch with me one hour?" Yet his disciples slept, when the cup was drank in the garden, and the agony endured alone. "He said sleep on now and take your rest;" so may you say. Christ will strengthen you henceforth to carry your cross alone. He prayed not to forget his wearied friends, or their welfare who increased his agony. He endured the suffering, despising the shame, poured out his life's blood amid desertion and false accusation.

You can not forget past manifestations, or cast them from you as unnecessary and dangerous if others do; for God is in them to you, for time and eternity. But this you can do, take your suffering, bleeding heart that lies slain and crushed in the dust, with all these manifestations, to Jesus. Cast them all into his bosom of love. Let him do or undo his own work; for what God has joined together, let no man put asunder. Let Jesus either strengthen or change these associations as he pleases and when he pleases; leave all with your advocate. He who suffered for man did not force his salvation upon man contrary to his choice; so you will not long be required to bestow your labor of love, where it will not meet with corresponding sympathy. Your work will change soon. Will you trust anew your cause with Jesus, who will not despise the broken and contrite heart, nor cast it from him, nor before others to be trampled upon by those who will then turn again and rend you. When one door is closed against you, another will be opened up into the narrowest narrow way, if you are faithful, which terminates nearer the throne than the way previously marked, for it is the martyr's way.

Consider the way and the desolate traveler, and learn what may be for thy comfort. This narrowest way is truly appalling to flesh and blood, without strong faith. With it, the heart is strong to endure, firm to sustain the consecrated cross. Without faith the stoutest heart might weary and sicken. Let us describe it in part.

CHAPTER III.

THE NARROW WAY.

THE traveler's course was suddenly obstructed. He was suddenly denounced by all as being deluded and led by Satan, and severely censured for doing, what a little time before, they insisted was a duty he owed to God and man.

He stood amazed at what he heard and saw; he began to reason, in what does my crime consist? Have not I earnestly sought to know the will of the Lord? Have I not reason, too, and just cause for receiving it from God, from the many incontrovertible proofs given me? Have not these efforts been blessed to the reclaiming and saving of souls, conscience also bearing me witness in the Holy Ghost that God requires this work at my hand?

While thus ruminating at the very juncture of the way, when this traveler most needed, it would seem, human sympathy, kindness and encouragement to meet the trials of the path previously marked out, he was ruthlessly stripped of all his props and helps in the seeming dark way, by the hands of those who had previously encouraged him to walk in this path; but now they wrapt their own reputation snugly in their self-vindicating garments, and flung the traveler disdainfully upon the ground, and trampled upon his reputation, feeling they were doing God's service.

Here I beheld an angel band take up the lonely, wounded traveler, and consoled him by saying, "Glory in your infirmities," self will here be slain. Enter this narrowest narrow way alone; it terminates nearest the throne. You need no such garments as those taken from you — such we call self-righteous garments. This way is so narrow, and the walls so high on either side, the traveler who walks this way can wear nothing that belongs to earth or self. He must carry no burdens. But before he enters this way, he must cast all into the sepulcher of Jesus, and become naked, that he may be clothed with garments of righteousness not his own. This garment is seamless. Its web is made of agony and love, its weft is Charity.

The traveler who makes progress in this narrowest narrow way, must go free from all impediments, that he may use both hands and feet. With his feet he shall tread upon scorpions and they shall not harm him; with his hands shall he readily embrace the cross, whether heavy or light, black or bloody. This way is full of crosses, large and small, that none but Christ's free men can raise. But naked faith, step by step can clear the way, and remove mountains of darkness and difficulties into the sea of God's love.

Remember faith is power. It comes by hearing — hearing by the Word of God. From the knowledge of God's faithfulness and love, and mercy and ability to perform all that he has promised, the power of faith laughs at impossibilities, and cries it shall be done.

Thus the traveler who sees the beginning of this narrow walk of faith, must, like Abraham, be sent out alone. Yet afterwards, when God proved him and tried him, and found him faithful, He said of him, I know my servant Abraham, he shall be called the friend of God. "He blessed him and multiplied him and said, thy seed shall be as the sand of the sea, and as the stars of heaven for multitude."

Notwithstanding this is the way cast up for the redeemed of the Lord to walk in, but few dare venture. If they do venture, many turn back because of the straightness and darkness of the way, choosing sight to faith. The walls of this way are so high, no light can strike the path direct to guide the feet, but light falls obliquely until the step is taken, then light and glory encircles head and heart.

Another thing I observed; the travelers, who made progress like Abel, Enoch, Elijah, Abraham, Moses and Elias, with many other worthies, felt the way with the heart, grasped the cross and the throne simultaneously, with the trusting, loving heart, and moved onward with a bold, firm step, "counting Him faithful who hath promised."

These travelers I beheld had but one eye. With that single eye they looked upward continually through the telescope of faith, which filled the body with light, instead of their pathway, which must be dark to the feet of faith. While the eye of faith, "beholding as in a glass, darkly," at first, but eventually, "face to face," "the glory of the Lord," insomuch they cry, stay the divine glory, until my capacity is enlarged.

The traveler who walks this way, can lean upon but

one heart, that is, the great heart of Infinite Love. "He may love many hearts as brethren," yet he must not lean upon any other. Then he feels no smitings — Love can not smite. Love feels no burdens he bears for his beloved. How easy to trust a heart you can love — how easy to love a heart you can trust.

"In the world ye shall have tribulation." From the ignorance and darkness of the human heart, it often unintentionally pierces and wounds when leaned upon, even when it would comfort. Not so with the heart that reposes in Jesus. "He said I have overcome the world, in me ye shall have peace." The heart that loves and trusts God, goes to him in every time of need and finds succor. The heart that trusts in self, or creature loves, goes to man with complaints. The soul that seeks for some friend instead of God, into whose bosom he can pour out his injuries, remains unblest, thus cherishing his wrongs by repetition and perpetuating them by dwelling upon them.

This state of things may be included among the tribulations ye shall have in the world, which spring out of human nature as it is. Thus it is written, "Offenses will come." But listen, Christ says, "I have overcome the world." He has marked out another path in the world which leads through the world, and yet is not of the spirit or love of the world, which if ye will walk in and abide in, ye shall find rest to your souls. "This is the victory even your faith." Whether ignorance or enmity prompts unkindness, it is the privilege of the man of faith to tread upon these scorpions, and his spirit feel no harm, even when his purest motives suffer.

MISUNDERSTANDINGS.

These are the scorpions which have stings and shall slay men. Misunderstandings cause hardness, coldness, reserve, distrust, finally suspicion of motives of those professing friendships. When this takes place, what a nest of vipers suddenly spring up and destroy for ever Christian love, influence and confidence. Thus the fair Eden of love is turned into the pandemonium of hell, often, too, on the very precincts of heaven.

The travelers in this narrow way, covered by the mantle of Charity and Love, obey the voice which says, "Be ye kindly affectioned one to another, in brotherly love, preferring one another."

This shall be a sign to those that believe, said Christ. "Behold, I give unto you power to tread upon serpents and scorpions, and over all the power of the enemy, and nothing shall by any means hurt you." "And if you drink any deadly thing, it shall not harm you."

In the world, or when you trust in the world, or any created ignorant being, "Ye shall have tribulation." "But be of good cheer, I have overcome the world." My victories are your victories, if you by faith lay hold upon my strength. They that overcome, shall walk with me in white, that is, in innocency, faith, purity and loving trust.

Now rally all your powers for noble strife with your mighty foes, defeat the machinations of Satan, which draw your mind to think and dwell upon the past; nor fear to trust the convictions of an honest mind, as to your duty to God and the world. This resistance of good impulses turns your purchased Eden into the prison of sorrow.

CHAPTER IV.

THE DOCTRINE OF ACCOUNTABILITY.

Turn your thoughts to another subject for a little moment.

Do you know what that book is which will be opened at the last day to every soul of man?

Listen; every thought, word and act of life is daguerreotyped upon space. Its moral character imaged there, accompanied with the divine approval, or disapproval. The good act brings a blessing to the soul — not the reward; *that* is laid up to be given hereafter. The sinful act brings reproof and condemnation — not the penalty; *that* too, comes after the judgment. The shadow of God's displeasure, which stands side by side with sin, is there daguerreotyped. The spirit may here feel, according to the law of influence of spirit upon spirit, the approval or disapproval of God towards present action. This may be at once inferred by the soul, if it watches for the shadow of displeasure or the smile of approval. How little do mortals realize, the purest and best, where self is not slain, when they vindicate themselves, how their account stands on yonder page, inscribed in characters of living fire; where the motive of each action is embodied in its true moral character, inscribed by the law of nature in imperishable letters, until "The heavens shall be rolled together as a scroll," to be burned up with the fervent heat of God's wrath, in love. Well might it be said, "The heavens are not pure in his sight," and his angels he chargeth with folly.

O, what events are recorded on yonder page of truth, of man and angel! "The heavens are not pure in his sight!"

Ques. Why?

Ans. There, in infinite space, stands the fearful record of man's life, and shall appear as it is, in judgment, "Whether it be good or evil."

"Every man's work shall be made manifest: for the day shall declare it, because it shall be revealed by fire; and the fire shall try every man's work, of what sort it is."

After the decisions of this great day, then shall the vast record be rolled up with the heavens as a scroll and be burned up; and the righteous shall dwell in the new earth, his sins being thus separated from him, "As far as the east is from the west," and for Christ's sake shall no more be brought to mind. While "the wicked shall be turned into hell, and all the nations that forget God," which is the second death.

Ques. Does not repentance blot these fearful records from the page of this book before the judgment?

Ans. No. But repentance brings the representation of God's forgiveness, which shows to assembled worlds, then as now, the sinner's sorrow for sin, and God's love and mercy in the plan of redemption.

These truths are plainly taught in God's Word, as the fact, but not the manner. Never before were mortals taught these truths, yet the word of angels is steadfast. Well might Paul say, in view of the deeds of the law, no flesh could be justified. O, the value of the redemption of Christ's purchased possession! Sell all, child of sorrow and want, and buy this field, this pearl of great price. Rejoice in this, that your name is written in the Lamb's Book of Life. Do you know what this book is? Precious, precious treasure! The Book of Life! yea Life!! bound up in one bundle of love with Christ in union and harmony with life, with love, life in love, love in life. Rejoice alway, yea I say rejoice, that your name is written in the Book of Life.

The covenant of faith made with Abraham, required of him sacrifices, watchings and sufferings. While yours is a covenant of death to self, and the gift of your powers to God. Then the new covenant of love, the white stone, the new name, the white robe, the bright morning star, shall dawn upon your soul in the deepest gloom of your future night of faith.

If this is not sufficient, all heaven shall be yours, if you will fight the good fight of faith, beat back Satan's strongest forces and honor God, yielding your powers to Him without reserve. "So fight the good fight of faith, finish your course, and keep the faith."

These trials have proved you true to God. You must forget your griefs and wrongs. God and angels are pleased. You have denied neither, though overwhelmed and amazed with grief. Your opposers must yet be slain to self, if saved to the uttermost. The crown of life shall be given to such as overcome. We have many things to say unto you, but you can not bear them now.

The higher manifestations, depend upon the strength

of your faith as to the time of their development. The preparation necessary, is discipline still, varied in forms. The manifestations are still the cross. The past manifestations and the manner they will be repeated and acted upon, will be the nails and spear to nail you to the cross. The circumstances of the past will aggravate your sufferings—the truth will be perverted by both the friends and enemies of the cross of Christ, which will throw great contempt upon the advocates of these unfolding mysteries based upon the law of mind, through the diversified ministrations of the Holy Spirit, and the media of angels sent by God to man.

The Lord will be avenged, for this they shall not prosper in their ways; yet you will suffer by it, suffer unjustly, suffer cruelly for the cause of truth. You will be charged with duplicity, heresy, blasphemy, as regardless of the most sacred, binding rites of the Christian faith, because you have been the channel of these spiritual developments — this shall be your last bitter cross. Then shall your sorrow on earth for ever end.

Ques. Must I drink of that bitter cup?

Ans. Not as God's wish, but Satan has done the deed through the spirit of sectarianism and pride of opinion in different minds, without investigation by some, lest they should be holden by their promises to the Lord to do what their hearts were not free to do, and by others, because more evil is, they say, developed in the world than good, from the present manifestations, not knowing the spirit of self is the source of attracting evil and that good lies back of the effects produced, which God designs to make manifest through the special providences of his grace.

Ques. What shall I say or do?

Ans. It shall be given you in that hour what to say. You will live to see a table spread in the sight of your enemies, of which they can not be permitted to eat.

"Tribulation worketh patience, patience experience, experience hope, hope maketh not ashamed."

Your faith in angelic ministrations and the Spirit's teachings, shall not make you ashamed in the judgment — neither let the truths taught make you fearful. What you know not now, you shall know hereafter. Receive with meekness the engrafted word of the Spirit, that ye may grow thereby.

What more can you, or any finite mind do, than to abandon all to God, to be led by the Spirit as he will, the manner being unknown to all but God. If you believe the Word of God, you are there promised protection, and to be led by the Holy Spirit into all truth. You are not required to give miraculous testimony, or expect assurances of that kind to convince others, but rest in God. If you do thus abandon yourself to his teaching, and do rely upon his Word without wavering, in small as well as great things, however adverse they may appear to human probabilities, quietly leave the result with God: all will be well.

Remember, doubt and fearfulness take the soul back again to first principles, destroy the foundation of hope and faith, make the soul unstable as water, vacillating as the wind, changing with appearances hither and thither, and resting no where. "These are clouds without water."

The soul without faith has no rest, is unfit for employment of any kind in heaven or on earth. Human faith is necessary to success in worldly enterprises. Faith in God is necessary to advancement in spiritual things. Plant your feet firm upon the rock of faith. When the winds blow, and the storms assail you, they shall only fix your feet more firmly upon the immutable truths of God's promises. Every succeeding storm will prove the stability of the foundation; there alone can the soul find rest. The past revelations of future good to those who walk uprightly, are sure as the foundations of heaven and earth. In these the writings correspond to the teachings of the Word.

The promises in the Bible are all conditional, and may be both literally and spiritually fulfilled to the man of faith, if, on his part, the conditions are met. Then, if it comes not (like faithful Abraham), wait its accomplishment, and stagger not at the tarrying or seeming non-fulfillment. It will come, it will not tarry.

Ques. Can man's free-agency prevent the fulfillment of events God has laid in his own wisdom? Will not the Lord finally overrule the purposes of man, and bring to pass just what will be for his own glory and man's best good?

Ans. In many ways the moral agency of man prevents the accomplishment of God's wise plans.

Repentance enables God, consistently with man's free-agency, to overrule disobedience, and finally accomplish the design of God in part.

Ques. When one has not intentionally done wrong, then how does it affect the plans of God?

Ans. To inconsiderately, or from ignorance, overlook duty, brings results as disastrous to the fulfillment of promises, as if the soul intended to do wrong. The neglect to know and practice the truth, furnishes no excuse for the ignorant, however honest. If the man is not moving in the divine order, he is opposing and preventing the designs of God as a moral agent. He that gathers not with him, scatters abroad. There is a wide difference between the permissive and special providences of God.

What is termed the permissive providences of God, should be regarded more as the effects of moral agency (which God will ever protect while he holds man responsible for his acts), than the will or good pleasure of the Lord, especially if the effects are evil.

Instance: A moral agent from ill will, murders your friend, fires your dwelling — or from carelessness or ignorance, or covetousness, so constructs machinery as to endanger and destroy life and property, the effect should be traced to the cause; all these things are prohibited by the law of love. God does not approve, or sanction, or second these acts; he hates oppression every where, yet is morally bound to protect moral agency, which is the image of God, in which man was first created. He comes not out against the transgressor to cut him off, until his cup of iniquity is full, until his race is run, however devastating his influence. At the same time, by his special providences, which are based upon the atonement, God comes to both parties — the injurer and the injured. The one is condemned, and sorrow of spirit is added with his fearful success in evil, while the other is comforted and sustained in spirit. The evil is overruled for their ultimate and eternal good, by the ever-watchful eye of God. Eternity, not time, is the promised place of recompense. Yet the awful deed is done, and is irreparable. Effect follows cause. Your friend is deprived of life, of influence, or of a home, by the agency of another, who has dared to violate the law of love.

This thwarts the purpose of God in giving life, possessions, and capabilities for usefulness to the murdered or injured man.

Again, the calamities which ignorance or neglect bring upon the community, or upon one individual, brings results as disastrous to God's will and pleasure, and the fulfilling of his wise purposes, as the other, if the same irredeemable results follow (*i. e.*), death and destruction. The only difference between the two is, the sin of intention to do wrong, lies heaviest upon the perpetrator, while the sin of the other is in proportion to his opportunity to know what was right. You see the results to the moral agent who commits the wrong, either through design or ignorance, differs, yet is the same in its effect, as to frustrating the will of the Lord towards the sufferer.

The calumniator, by destroying the reputation of an innocent, virtuous man, prevents his usefulness among his fellow-men, and thwarts the purposes of God towards him, and through him the world is robbed of a blessing, by the untimely setting of such moral suns.

Man is highly culpable for his neglect to know and practice the truth, when his every act affects his own destiny, and the well-being of the human family, directly or indirectly, and either honors or dishonors God.

Cause and effect are ordained of God in spiritual life, as well as in the physical universe. The effect of evil can only be averted by reformation and obedience.

CHAPTER V.

LIGHT ON THE NARROW WAY.

Ques. WHY do I not gain greater victory over my trials? Why is my mind so held here, when I try to dismiss all?

Ans. Self still breathes, Satan is not steadfastly resisted. This fact portrays your spiritual state. This should teach you to give up all for Christ. To keep all upon the altar of sacrifice, includes every thing. Satan tries to hold your mind to dwell upon the past. Resist Satan steadfastly, lest he breathe again upon the slain to self and sin, and they revive. Remember the spiritual law of life is the same in evil as in good. When the soul obeys the law of love, it walks not after the flesh but after the Spirit. Christ breathed upon his disciples, and said receive the Holy Ghost, and they live the resurrection life of faith. If the soul neglects to resist Satan's wiles, *he* breathes upon them the spirit of self and unbelief, sin revives, the soul dies to good, or as some would term it, backslides.

The abandonment of self includes many things. First, the thoughts, desires, affections, and all the powers of soul and body. Your duty is simply to turn away from all temptation, not to dwell upon any thing but God's will to you in present duty. "Sufficient unto the day is the evil thereof."

Ques. Why do I not obtain greater light upon these mysterious developments?

Ans. Cease from all painful anxiety upon that point; truth will be developed little by little, as you can digest it. Let friends say and think as they will. Think it not strange that God has led you in so trying a path, just as your sun was about to set, causing you so much trial, contempt and suffering, involving you deeper and deeper in mystery, instead of vindicating and delivering you at once. "All things shall work together for good to them that love God."

Your dark walk of faith, if you finally overcome Satan's forces against you, will be the brightest star in your crown of rejoicing. The reward will hereafter a thousand times overbalance the satisfaction you would have here enjoyed, without this trial of your faith and patience. Look back, see that already, before this cup was given you, you have been tried upon almost every point to which human life is incident, to crucify you to the world, and make you a partaker of His holiness. Whom He loveth He chasteneth, if they will not otherwise part with their idols. The wind has always been "tempered to the shorn lamb." This is your last severe trial. When you have overcome this and feel willing to follow Christ through evil report as well as good, and glory in your humiliation and desertion of all but God, then the trials which will follow will be borne in patient submission.

The conflict will be ended — the victory will be won through the blood of the Lamb. God will be honored and the power of the Son be manifest in you, if you overcome the world, the flesh, and the devil. There will be greater joy in heaven among the saints and angel throng, if you, a child of sorrow, in affliction, in weakness and without human consolation and encouragement (such as others have), resist steadfastly Satan's fiery darts, and endure the opposition of the world to this mysterious manner of the Spirit's work assigned you, in bringing before the world in this light the Bible truth of Angelic Ministrations, the offices of the Holy Spirit and the death of self. The baptism of the believer into Christ's death, the renewal and restoration of the human powers into the name and nature of the Father, Son, and Holy Ghost. That mind, when passively yielded, may be led by the Holy Spirit into all truth.

If you presevere in the narrowest narrow way from choice, you will reap an hundred-fold in this life, and in the world to come life everlasting.

Ques. How may I know, these promises will be fulfilled?

Ans. The suggestions of the Holy Spirit are as infallible as His word — if obeyed in faith are as sure of fulfillment as the Bible promises.

I have told you, said Jesus, that when it comes to pass ye might believe.

Ques. Am I not liable to be deceived by the suggestions of Satan, or my own mind instead of the Spirit?

Ans. Not deceived, if you try the spirits.

Ques. By what standard may I know the Spirit's teachings?

Ans. The Holy Spirit originates holy desires to promote the glory of God, to the utter nothingness of self, and is always accompanied by faith in God. To the eye of sense, the work of the Spirit is always mysterious, beyond nature and above nature—that is the reason the aid of the Spirit is promised to man, to do for man what man can not do for himself. If the soul could please God in his fallen condition without the Spirit helping his infirmities, the Holy Spirit would never have been given, for God never performs a superfluous act of any kind. The Spirit's operation is mainly upon the heart, influencing it through the affections, the will and the understanding. The earnest of the Spirit, is present faith in the things presented, and a desire to possess them, because God wills it.

The faith of assurance is a satisfactory rest the mind realizes in expecting the things promised, with patience accompanying it, to wait God's time for its fulfillment, as the best time. The spirit, the heart, the mind, are terms used in Scripture to signify the individual trinity of man, while the living soul signifies the whole man entire.

This figure represents the circle of time and eternity. How valueless will be the opinions of men when you step from the circle of time into eternity.

Soon the hand that traces these lines will be cold in death. Those eyes will weep no more. Your throbbing head and aching heart will be hushed in the silence of death.

When your spirit will go to its reward, if found clothed, to receive the smile of well done, there you will not heed or need human sympathy — bearing palms of victory, clothed in light, your works will follow.

These written words shall penetrate into the hearts of those that now reject these manifestations as a dangerous error and a delusion of Satan.

You must speedily be clothed, that you may be perfect, entire, wanting nothing to complete the work. Shrink not from the cross; it is the way to thrones and dominions; love the precious cross; die upon the cross for the cause of truth; desire to know nothing but Christ, and him crucified.

Your time is comparatively short — work while it is day. O, improve your precious time! Give yourself to the work of preparation. How soon you will suffer for the last time, and pray for the last time for a lost world.

You should regard it a privilege to suffer for Christ, to watch, to pray. You should feel your own helplessness; this drives you to the strong for strength, to the wise for wisdom.

Do nothing, say nothing, that you can not present to the judgment seat, at the judgment day.

Be ye holy. Be perfect even as your Father in heaven is perfect.

Let no man deceive you by saying the promises of God were to primitive saints, not to the whole world.

Greater works than these shall ye do, said Jesus, because I go to my Father.

What I say unto you, I say unto all, watch, rest in God. Yea, rest from your own works, as God did from his. Let God work in you to will and do his good pleasure; let him originate every desire; let him do the work through you.

CHAPTER VI.

THE DEATH OF SELF.

Oct. 3*d*, 1852.—I. *Ques.* WILL the Lord give me an increase of light upon the manifestations of the past, and my duty and my privilege in spiritual things?

Ans. Do you now, from choice, wholly abandon yourself to the teachings of the Holy Spirit as promised through Christ from the Father? And will you no more look to man for the wisdom that cometh from above, but endeavor in spirit to wait upon Christ, believing what the Word of God teaches, and the Spirit when it agrees with the Word, no more doubt or fear being misled, but by the power of the will trust in God, cease from self and others? If so, by the power of the Spirit you shall be kept from error, from sin, from self, from idols, and continually rest in God's great heart of love. That while you thus trust, you shall never loose the present light you have, but continually increase in the love and knowledge of God, day by day, until Christ shall remove you to higher joys, to brighter scenes of vision and spiritual delights.

Your days of mourning for sin shall end, your sun shall no more set, nor your moon withdraw her light. This is the covenant that I will make with my chosen in the last days: "I will sprinkle clean water upon them, and cleanse them from all their idols, and from all filthiness of the flesh and spirit. I will write my new law in their hearts, and in their minds will I print it. And I will be to them a God, and they shall be to me a people. Then one shall not say to another, know ye the Lord, for all shall know Him, from the least to the greatest."

Human teaching will give place to divine teaching, which will preach to the hearts and minds of all, that man shall no more glory in man, but they shall say, God has written upon my heart his new best name of love. He has put his spirit within me, and now I do know of the doctrine, whether it be of God or Antichrist.

The four ways we told you, previously, self was pointing to, are now crucified.

You must look alone to God to be directed, resisting all solicitations from Satan to doubt God's willingness or power to keep you. Do not limit the Holy One of Israel in your heart; let him have room to breathe and move and stir, and he will be your life in all future time. The promises made you shall be literally fulfilled, in God's own time, if the conditions are met.

Desire not to have your deliverance hastened. God's time is the best time — wait upon God in faith, nothing doubting, with thanksgiving and praise.

You have nothing to fear, God will open another door when this is closed. The way is plain before you, though faith sees through a glass darkly and hopes against hope.

The future will reveal to you great things, both of sufferings and victories. Yet "your peace shall be like a river, and your righteousness like the waves of the sea."

Think not because you suffer in agony of spirit, that self reigns. Christ's sufferings did not arise from selfishness in his own heart, but from the unbelief and sins of others. You must drink of his cup in spirit, and feel in

NOTE EXPLANATORY OF DRAWING SECOND.

The original of the opposite sketch was, like the preceding, drawn in the spring of 1852, as a representation of what the writer must meet with in the performance of the work assigned her in this manifestation, not so much from the world at large, as from her most intimate Christian friends and the Christian world as a whole, among whom her influence and reputation would be as effectually crucified and slain, for a time, as though she was nailed to a cross for crime.

The original figure was represented as a bare skeleton upon the cross, stripped of clothing and flesh, to portray to her mind she must not expect human sympathy or helps, but naked and alone she must obey the voice of the Spirit, and reduce to practical experience the Christian theory to die to self and the world, in order to follow Christ in newness of life, even when and where there was none to lead but the Holy Spirit, as the Church should condemn this manner of the Spirit's teachings.

This thought so overwhelmed her, she laid aside the original drawing, before it was finished, for some weeks, until some members of her family urged her to complete it. Other figures were given as also suffering crucifixion or death in various forms in the nineteenth century. The writer failed to understand by the original what the present drawing explains, which was recently given by the same influence upon the hand, changing the form somewhat by covering the figure, and instead of suspending it between the heavens and the earth, as before, placing it upon a platform, supported on one side by Faith and Love, and on the other by Hope and Charity, then the whole was encircled with a sweep of the pencil from Charity to Hope, representing Charity as the crowning grace of all the graces,

> The bond of perfectness,
> The garb that saints must wear,
> Who war no more
> 'Gainst God or man,

while the figure represents all those who have suffered with Christ in being led by the Spirit, since the descent of the Holy Spirit upon Christ at his baptism, as stated in the written explanations accompanying the drawing, likewise all who will suffer with Him for being thus led, until His second appearing.

This figure represents all who will be led by the Holy Spirit, instead of the popular theology of the times, in every country, since the descent of the Holy Spirit upon Christ at his baptism.

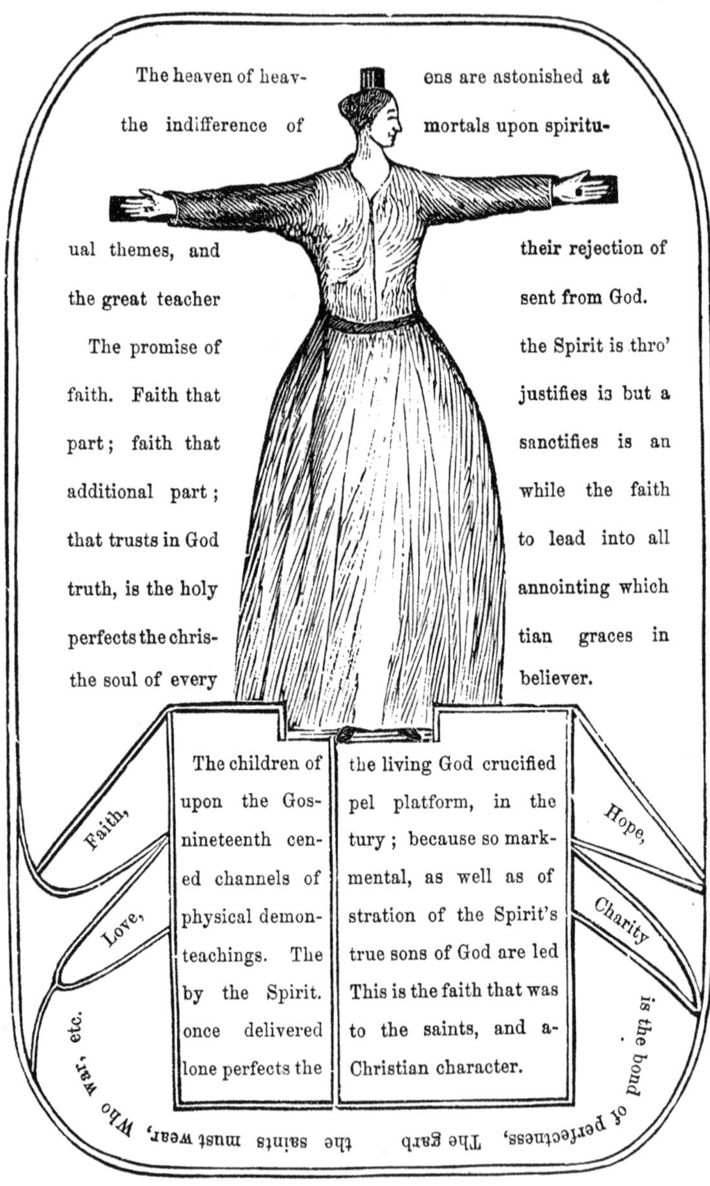

Verily shall Christ find faith on the earth when he comes the second time, without a sin offering.

a degree what he felt, if you would reign with him. How else could you drink of his cup, unless by a similarity in circumstances. His own disciples and friends forsook him. He went alone into the judgment hall, to be questioned by his enemies. Think of this: He offered his love, this was despised; and they said, away with this vile fellow; he hath a devil! and in their hate, plotted his death, and took his life. They saw no beauty in the humble Nazarine, "That they should desire him," and in their contempt, said, crucify him!

When you have passed the changes which are to be the tests of your covenant, "Then shall your light go forth as brightness, and your salvation as a lamp that burneth."

"Thy Maker is thy husband," to guide, sustain and provide for thee here; and when thy release comes, Heaven shall furnish you with a home, with bright robes, brightened by every trial of your faith; with palms of victory in your hand, shall you join in the song of songs, "Worthy, worthy is the Lamb that was slain, who hath redeemed us by his own blood."

Now will you faint, when misrepresented, condemned, accused, because others reject and deny the possibility of your being thus led by God? If you do, this glory will depart and be given to another, who will from the heart serve the living God.

Rest in God without desire, only seek to do his will, as angels do in heaven. They feel no desire for this or that, but cheerfully do the will of God, as his will is made known by the daily providences of God, both in heaven and on earth.

Do you suppose angels and the departed know all, or any of the future, only as the Holy Spirit reveals it unto them?

The Sonship or created humanity of Christ, and the angels of glorious light (Scripture declares), knew not the future, "But of that day and that hour knoweth no man, no, not the angels which are in heaven, neither the Son, but the Father." Yet the Holy Spirit knows, for he is the Spirit of light and truth. No created nature was attached to his mission, for he is spirit, and only adapted to spirit — is only discerned by the spirit of men and angels. Christ appears in heaven now, as he did on earth, in form of body, to represent his mission to the world of mankind. The cross and the sepulcher are the throne of his glory, and proclaims a crucified and risen Lord on earth, and in hell, and in heaven. He made the offering of himself once by death, now he ever liveth to give life, eternal life, to all who seek.

Do you not see the difference here? The death of the body reconciled all to God, by slaying the Man of Sin, and placed the human family in a condition to receive life. This risen life is offered to the world by faith in Christ. Therefore how vain will be the hope of all those who depend upon the merits of Christ's death for life, unless they choose and seek, and by faith "eat of his body" (which is truth), and "drink of his blood" (which is life), in love of the truth? This condition of salvation is adapted to man's free moral agency. Thus Jesus said, "Verily, verily, I say unto you, except ye eat the flesh of the Son of Man, and drink his blood, ye have no life in you."

The infant world are saved by virtue of this life being embodied in humanity. The untaught, neglected, ignorant man, is weighed in an even balance of mercy and justice, according to his works, his light, his privileges. Here is the field for Christian effort. Man should be deeply instructed in the way of life. For this purpose his faculties are developed slowly; the senses are adapted to his perceptions, as channels to the soul.

Man is ignorant, when born, of both good and evil. His nature is sinful, because the spirit of self is inherited from Satan. This is the legacy of Satan to man, by man's free choice, which he transmits to his posterity, because he refuses to be saved from all sin, and part with all his idols. Scripture teaches, if ye believe, then are your children holy. How few, with Abraham, claim the promise of the covenant, and transmit their holiness to their posterity, instead of sin. The redemption of Christ made provision for the entire renewing of the nature of man in the embryo!* The human nature of Jesus Christ was never selfish, therefore he must save man from sin, not in sin. "For sin he condemned sin in the flesh;" there sin must be parted with before he can be raised with Christ in newness of life. The flesh signifies the carnal mind; this is the body of death Christ delivers from.

The partially saved, have still unbelief and self in the soul. "Precious in the sight of the Lord is the death of his saints." This death of the carnal mind is what is so precious in the sight of the Lord, not the death of the natural body, for that is the effect of sin. "Death has passed upon all men, for that all have sinned." Christ delivers not absolutely from natural death, but died himself, and delivers from the death of sin. "The carnal mind is enmity against God." He gained victory over enmity, death, hell and the grave.

* See Appendix, Note C., Doctrine of Transmission, as explanatory of this subject.

There is nothing valuable in Christ's view of the effect of sin on the soul or body of man. "Yet the righteous hath hope in his death," because Christ is the resurrection and the life.

Death is gloomy in its nature; its work is taking down the tabernacle by suffering and disease, which God never designed to be destroyed. Death is solemn; it marks the progress of evil in the world. The body of this death of the carnal mind is to be desired. Such a death is precious in the sight of the Lord, and no other.

Death in this sense, is the entrance into life. The death of the body does not change man's moral nature, it changes his circumstances. The death of the carnal mind alone changes man's nature, and is the beginning of life from the dead — a life which never ends. Its vital elements are love and faith, so it remains when man passes into the spirit world. In no sense is man's nature changed by natural death, only his circumstances.

Man being saved by faith, still lives by faith, for without faith man or angel could not please God. Therefore the Apostle said, "The life which I now live in the flesh, I live by the faith of the Son of God."

A life without faith, is the life of the worldling, which ends in the second death, but not the eternal life of immortality. Heaven, without faith, would soon be turned into hell. The want of faith in exercise between man and man, makes the social circle a den of vipers. Love and faith would turn hell into heaven, the lion in rage to a lamb in spirit. Such are some of the effects of faith in man and upon the destiny of man.

The effects of faith in heaven are still more glorious. It is the channel of spiritual knowledge there, and aids the sight, as the senses did the faith here. Faith here comes by hearing; man beholds here, as in a glass, the glory of the Lord, darkly, but then face to face. This vision does not preclude the necessity of faith in God, and between angel and angel, any more than beholding the image or likeness of a friend, precludes the necessity of cherishing confidence in that friend when you meet. Mutual happiness of parties, depend upon their mutual faith in each other. Professions of faith and love are as valueless to God as to man. He who sees the heart knows its true state, and man meets with the same degree of love and confidence from God, as he reposes in God.

So the same of evil and unbelief. God values man according to what he really is, not according to what he seems to be.

The love of the intellect is required, the love of reason is also necessary. The love of all the affections is the base of joy. The love of the mind, might and strength, belongs to God.

Mechanical instead of affectional obedience to the requirements of the law of love, when the heart is estranged, is an insult to God, as well as between man and man. Professed friendship, because necessity or policy requires it, is obnoxious to justice, and pierces the soul more than open enmity. Man can not value a friendship because it is to the interest of the party to profess it. God loves the cheerful giver, so does the man of God. Never rely upon or trust friendships which only seek to serve self in the union. Friendships without heart affection, are like snow in summer and rain in harvest.

CHAPTER VII.

THE DEATH OF THE BODY CONTRASTED WITH THE DEATH OF SELF.

Oct. 9, 1852.—I. *Ques.* FROM the teachings of last night, I desire to inquire still further upon the subject of death. It was written, death was gloomy—death was solemn. Should the Christian regard death as gloomy?

Ans. God is life, holiness, happiness. All that is opposed to the nature of God, can not increase the happiness of his creatures. Yet God can, by the power of his grace, bring good out of evil, and in this sense, it may be said, it is better to die than to live, since man is a sufferer from the effects of sin. Yet death is gloomy and sorrowful in its separation of ties. The helpless family is left without the parent's care. The parent, like the lightning-scathed oak, is bereft of its branches, which God gave him to beautify his house, and add strength, power and numbers to his individual community, in imitation of his Creator.

Sin is the cause of death—death is the effect of sin. God is the author of life. By virtue of this life in humanity, he saves from the second death. By virtue of his giving his life on the cross, he reconciled the world to God, and saves from sin through his obedience (*viz.*), from the death of the carnal mind. By virtue of his resurrection from the dead, he saves man, soul and body, who believes in him. He hath said, "I am the resurrection and the life." Because of sin, it may be said, the day of their death is better than the day of their birth. This can only be said of the righteous. "Woe unto the wicked, it shall be ill with him."

Ques. May I ask if the happiness of the soul is not greatly enhanced, that has hope in his death?

Ans. The fact that he has suffered death, does not enhance his happiness. The change in his circumstances, which Christ brings out by delivering from sorrow in the body, is a happiness to the soul, through the life of Christ alone; not the death of the body, for the wicked die. Therefore the Apostle said, "To live is Christ, to die in him is gain."

Christ is the eternal life. That life you may live here, if by the power of the will you surrender the carnal life of sin for the true life of God. Look alone to this source for all your happiness.

When death comes, meet it calmly, trusting alone in the promise of God in Christ, "That because he lives, ye shall live also." The grave is the house of the living. The resurrection is the triumph of the cross of Christ over death and the grave.

How unwise for souls to think at death a moral change will be mechanically wrought, making the sinner holy, and leave the work until that hour, of being made one in Christ, in newness of life, as though there was virtue in the curse of death which sin brought upon man. These are the traditions of men. Jesus said, "O, Father, I pray not that thou shouldst take them out of the world, but that thou shouldst keep them from the evil." God hath said, "Keep my commandments, that your days may be long upon the earth."

God delighteth in the death of his saints, when they die to sin; and when the body dies he will receive them to himself.

He also greatly delights in their long lives of holiness and usefulness, that the world may know by these the power of grace to sanctify them through the word of truth, to keep them from evil, that God may be glorified in the work of his Son in them, giving life to the dead, "That where I am, there may they be also." This is the Christian's hope, the resurrection and the life. O precious hope! it reaches to that within the vale, whither Christ, your forerunner, is gone. Look and live.

CHAPTER VIII.

THE SOUL'S TRUE LIFE.

Oct. 12, 1852.—I. *Ques.* I DESIRE to know what is the resurrection life, referred to by the Spirit's teachings, that I may seek it understandingly.

Ans. This life has but one eye, one desire, one aim, one work — to glorify God.

Self has many desires, many eyes, many aims, many kinds of work. All this is not of God. Self may be mixed with good desires — as chemical properties may be mixed, without uniting in affinity and forming a new compound, each retaining its own natural inherent powers — and the effort to make them unite is fruitless, because opposed most absolutely to each other; the one must overcome the other. Self must give place to holiness, or holy desires will give place to self. Self is abundant in works for its own praise. Self loves to do good works to get praise. Self will stimulate the feeble and timid to great acts of self-denial and valor, that the world may behold their zeal for God. And in this way they glorify themselves, and censoriously condemn all others. When they speak of what others neglect to do, they invariably contrast their own works, saying, I have done thus and so,— Pharisee like — I thank thee I am not as other men. I have done much for the cause of God and truth. Such are full of desires, curious, self-seekers, and of sectarian glory. These emotions readily unite with self, and form a new compound, unlike the worldling, unlike the pure in heart, the saved from self. (These are the godly without Christ Jesus).

Those who have risen with Christ in the true sense of the resurrection life, become dead indeed to sin, and alive to God, have no more care about the reputation of self, no curiosity to know the opinions of the world in reference to their course, or the result of their works in faith. They cease from desire. Their eye is single, steadfastly beholding God in Christ in every thing happening to them. They passively rest in spirit, for God is in them in newness of life. They confidently lay hold upon infinite strength to work his will in all things, in his own time, and in his own way. This way is the lowly, meek way, that hides pride from man. "Woe unto him that all men speak well of," for such seek to please the world, not God. The godly in Christ Jesus shall suffer persecution. Ye are not of the world, therefore the world hateth you. None can be more innocent and harmless than the One who never lifted up His voice or made a cry in the streets, than "He who was led as a lamb to the slaughter," and was before his shearers dumb—He opened not his mouth; who performed all his works for the good of others, and pleased not himself; but his pleasure was in doing the will of the Father. Yet Jesus was persecuted, crucified, despised and rejected of men.

"Strait is the gate, and narrow is the way that leads to life." The way is no wider than the footprints of

Jesus. "He is the way." The way leads through every man's heart; if he will only seek to find it, he may easily do so. The portals of his door are marked with blood. Jesus' footsteps linger there, waiting for admission. "Behold," he says, "I stand at the door and knock; If any man open the door, I will come in and sup with him, and he with me," and the feast shall be everlasting love. There is only one way to the straight gate, that is the narrow way of life through the heart, which slays self, then sinks into the immensity of God.

Oct. 16, 1852.—II. *Ques.* Have I right feelings in reference to the providences of God to me?

Ans. The right feeling is to receive all with patience and thankfulness, however mysterious, contradictory and dark, and say, glorify thyself, O, God! in this dark dispensation to me.

The feeling of your sorrows is no evidence you are not right, nor that others are doing right or wrong. You must feel your trials, or they would not be trials to you. This belongs to human nature. Jesus felt his sorrows more than any man, because he was more pure than any man. Wrongs are felt in proportion to purity; the power to bear wrongs, is in proportion to innocency. This you will find true in all minds, divine and human.

The Holy Spirit is a gentle, tender spirit, while the selfish, proud heart is obstinate. The true, tender, sensitive heart, is a sure evidence of purity, innocency and justice. Mark the difference between sensitiveness and suspicion and distrust.

The sensibilities of the human nature of Jesus were not blunted by cruelty, or hardened bv sin. Not so of man, who is under the power and dominion of self, in alliance with Satan, filled with suspicion and distrust, evil surmising and evil speaking and false accusation. The attributes of the Father, Son and Holy Spirit are the same in essence and divinity. The family above is assimilated into the same spirit of love, as members of the same body. The family of Christ on earth must also possess the same divine nature, be of a tender, charitable, loving, gentle spirit. Be sensitive to sin, to wrongs of all descriptions, as a safeguard against the indulgence of sin and of wrongs to others.

Those who are taught by the Spirit to respect the rights of all, are the little ones Christ speaks of, that it were better to have a millstone tied about the neck, and the man cast into the sea, than to offend one of these little ones. Offend means to injure, or cause to be ill treated, persecuted, falsely accused. Such are to Christ as the apple of the eye. This tender spirit belongs to human nature, as it came from the hands of its Maker. This nature was in agony in the Garden, prayed while the disciples slept. Angels came and strengthened Jesus, inasmuch as he was made a little lower than they, for the purpose of suffering and death.

Satan in man, is the accuser of the brethren. When the conscience condemns, never cover it, but remove all cause of condemnation immediately; never rest or sleep with a sense of guilt resting upon you.

Again we say, when conscience acquits, hold yourself innocent before man and God, keeping your conscience void of offense before God and man, purifying the heart by obeying the truth. The consciousness of right is limited to knowledge. You can only judge as you know in spiritual things, as in temporal. God is not a hard master, condemning the soul for what it can not do or can not know. So long as you do the best you know, you are innocent. When new light is given, it requires obedience in proportion to knowledge.

"Precious in the sight of the Lord is the death of his saints." Die to self, in an evil conscience, or heart of unbelief.

PART SECOND.

LAWS OF THE SPIRITUAL MANIFESTATION.

CHAPTER IX.

THE LAW OF AFFINITY.

PREVIOUS to the date of the second chapter, July 17, 1852, some thirty pages were given, not alluded to in my journal, which were taken by some person from my room, which I have never found.

Nov. 30*th*, 1852.—I. *Subject continued from missing papers.*—Some additional facts, in connection with past lessons, explaining the law of mind as developed by this manifestation, will now be given.

Christ, who undertook the redemption of man from sin and death, is not limited in ways and means to effect his purpose. He deviseth his own plans and executeth them, teaching in his Word there are diversities of gifts, but the same spirit. And there are differences of administrations but the same Lord.

And there are diversities of operations, but it is the

same God which worketh all in all. But the manifestation of the Spirit is given to every man to profit withal. The spirit of prophesy and the gift of tongues, the gifts of healing, were not for the individual alone, but as a sign to the people that God was speaking to them through the organs of clay.

This manifestation of the Spirit was given to profit the world, not to supercede the gospel of repentance and faith in Christ, nor to be despised by the world of darkness on spiritual things. The spirit of prophesy was for the believer, the gift of tongues for the people.

All the works of God are governed by fixed laws on earth, in hell, in heaven. Law signifies penalty and protection. Spirit and matter are the subjects of this law. The law governing the spirit world is spiritual, and must be discerned by the Spirit. The effect of the laws governing the material world, which are termed physical, may be discerned by the intellect.

In the preceding lessons you inquired by what power or force your hand was moved. The answer was, by the motive power of spirit upon the nervous system. You inquired, what is motive power? The answer was, the force of organic life. That when the dynamic force of spiritual manifestations was better understood, the chaff would be separated from the wheat. That the true exegesis of the law controlling the manifestation, would establish it upon a sound, philosophical, practical, biblical basis, giving another exhibition of the love and mercy of God in Christ to apostate man.

This organic life originated in the Deity, was the law of union between the Father, Son, and Holy Spirit, between the humanity and divinity of Christ, between

Christ and the believer, between good finite, and God infinite, between the soul and body, spirit and matter, between mind and mind, spirit and spirit, good and good, evil and evil.

It is transfused through all matter and all space. It is the mysterious power between the mineral and vegetable kingdom, that causes vegetation to spring up out of the earth, and nourishes animal life; the mystery of propagation in the animal kingdom. It is the life and vitality of light and heat, of air and water.

It is the connecting link between spirit and matter, earth and heaven, time and eternity, and holds the vast universe of worlds in space.

If such is the power of one element in the law of mind, how great is the mind from which this element emanates, that is so vast and wonderful and powerful in its effects upon all the works of God.

How deep the design of God in man's creation; how great the price he paid for man's redemption; how glorious the habitation prepared for man's reception.

How just and good the law conducting man to that higher home of love and rest; yet all this is slighted, rejected, neglected by the mass of mankind, made for such high destinies. "What is man that thou art mindful of him, or the Son of Man that thou visitest him!"

This influence which we call motive power, originating in God, like faith and love, was uncreated, and was given to man and angel to promote their usefulness and happiness, and is an element in mind, and in the spiritual influence controlling mind.

To make the subject plain, we will contrast the hidden laws of spiritual life, with the physical laws controlling the material world, which are known only in their effects, by affinity and attraction, adhesion, cohesion and gravitation, with their centripetal and centrifugal forces.

Remember, in all the teachings of Christ, he used literal subjects to illustrate spiritual things. Man in his spiritual nature is a subject of the spiritual law of God. This law is adapted to man's free moral agency.

This life-moving power, controlling mind, is faintly perceived by man. This law is an emanation from the perfections of the Godhead. Obedience, then, to this law, is the perfection of wisdom. The fear of the Lord is the beginning of wisdom. To obey him, is wisdom perfected. You see then it is not an unnecessary, arbitrary law, but a law of love, adapted to man's spiritual wants and nature. All spiritual intelligences were created holy, and were the legitimate offsprings and subjects of the spiritual law of life. Sin changed their natures, but not the law of life. Therefore existence and intelligence is based upon this law of life. Hence the free-agency of man, and the power of evil works death if not resisted.

The dynamic force or motive power of spirit, of both good and evil, demonstrated in the manifestation, may be illustrated by the element of electricity in nature —its power of communication developed through the galvanic battery. The power in motion possessing affinities with the surrounding element in nature, attracts by this power of affinity, sufficient electric force to conduct the fluid to its opposite pole.

The dynamic power of the machine which gives motion, illustrates the law controlling matter in the manifestion. The affinity existing between the battery and the electricity in nature, illustrates the spiritual affinities existing between mind in the body and spirits in the spirit world.

That according to fixed laws controlling mind, for the safety and preservation of mind, the good attract the good and repel the evil. When the mind parts with its evil for the good, it becomes good, then the good attracts and assimilates into its own likeness. Thus it is written, if ye are like Him, ye shall see Him as He is, and be changed into his image from glory to glory.

It is through this element of mind or motive power, the passive spirit is renewed and sanctified. "Draw nigh to God, and he will draw nigh to you. If ye forsake him, he will cast you off for ever."

On the same principle does evil attract evil; hand joins in hand. Satan is the principle of evil in both worlds. The spirit of self is identical with the spirit of Satan. It is Satan's stronghold in the human soul, it is Satan's food, Satan's seat, Satan's empire.

The spirit of self in man attracts evil to itself, from the evil of the spirit world. This spiritual law of mind which is illustrated in the nature of the facts obtained, should claim the attention of the wise and unwise, rather than the productions of writers, until the law is better understood and the writers are holy. The analogy between the fixed laws controlling mind and the fixed laws controlling matter, may be illustrated still further. Affinity in minds is the basis of fellowship and friendships. Attraction in matter, illustrates sympathy, agreeableness, suitableness, congeniality in spirit. Kindred minds unite by the same law of attraction as matter, when mind comes in contact with mind, on a short acquaintance. There is in minds similarly constituted, an irresistible approval and attraction, that renders the stranger at once agreeable.

Adhesion and cohesion in matter illustrates the fidelity, loyalty and strength of love for friends, country and God. This being the first principle in harmony with spiritual law and the Great Giver of the law of mind: adhering to His precepts, sticking unto His testimonies, resisting separation, cohering unto that which is good.

The law of gravitation in nature, illustrates the motive power of the law of love as given in the Gospel. Its innate power and tendency in drawing bodies to their center, illustrates the centripetal force and power of faith to draw all men to the Father, their true center of life through Christ, "That whosoever believeth on Him shall have eternal life." It also represents the necessity of obedience to fixed laws of mind as well as in matter. Should matter cease to obey her laws, as mind has, results the most disastrous would follow.

The law of repulsion illustrates the disunion of opposed bodies and principles, of good and evil, and their incapacity to unite. It also illustrates the doom of the sinner, wandering from his true orbit or path of duty. By rebellion he is cast out into outer darkness, by the centrifugal force of repulsion. The law of vegetation in nature, is also illustrative of the resurrection of the body.

Time is a shadow of eternity. The material universe with its innumerable worlds, is the shadow or emblem of the spirit world, with its many mansions prepared for the righteous. The laws governing the material world is a representation of fixed laws controlling spiritual life.

Learn from the book of nature, the first great principles of the law controlling mind. Learn to study God in the revelation of himself in his works, his providences, his Word, through the telescope of faith and prayer. Learn to obey the laws of life and health, lest you convert the best gifts of God into missiles of disease and death. Learn to obey the spiritual law of your spiritual nature, that you may live and honor the Son, as the Son honored the Father.

Faith comes by hearing, and hearing by the Word of God. When mind understands its high destiny and the right cultivation of its powers, the gospel of truth will take deeper root in the soil of the mind, breaking league with sin and Satan, and presenting to the eye of the Redeemer the goodly fruit, like unto the trees of righteousness planted by the rivers of waters, whose leaves shall not wither, and which bringeth forth its fruit in its season.

Divine wisdom is the parent tree of true philosophy, planted in the eternity of God, sending forth its branches throughout heaven and earth laden with the fruit of life. Its fruit is not forbidden, but man and angel, and the highest archangel are invited to the feast.

All knowledge gained from this source will increase the happiness and usefulness of the saved in heaven. Therefore the motive power of truth should prompt man to search for wisdom as for hid treasure, and when he has found it, bind it about his neck as an ornament, hold it fast and not let it go; for it shall be as a talisman to life, and health to the soul. Then when thy hand has plucked the fruit of life, eat and digest it, that thy threefold life may be developed in time to join the goodly company of angels, who kept their first estate with patriarchs and prophets and apostles and martyrs and saints, where the redeemed and the Redeemer of man meet in common brotherhood to celebrate the marriage supper of the Lamb. Christ will then drink anew of the wine with his bride, the Church, that he has redeemed from among every nation, kingdom and tongue, from the great family of earth.

Man will find true philosophy the healthful life-current of both soul and body, bearing away on its calm, temperate bosom of truth, the sophistries of all falsities, in man's physical, moral and spiritual developments, until the spirit of progressive intelligence becomes united by the mission of spiritual philosophy, with the natural life-current of the parent tree, wisdom.

Nov. 1852.—II. *Ques.* What is truth, and what is true philosophy, and what is my duty in the writings, since I am so ignorant, and every thing is still clothed in so much mystery?

Ans. God is truth. Light is truth. The Holy Spirit that lighteneth every man that cometh into the world, is truth. The truth makes free. To walk in him and abide in the truth is your duty.

The truth in the writings is covered by its advocates as well as its opposers, with false philosophy and sophistries of perverted minds. The premises and conclusions of both are wrong.

Man is so earthly and groveling in his affections and aspirations, so sectarian in his investigations, he at once converts the best gifts of God into selfish temples of worship to serve the mammon of unrighteousness, perverting the best gifts of God to their own destruction.

This manifestation is a branch of spiritual philosophy, demonstrated by its effect upon the passive hand, while the brain or mind, the only medium of thought, is left unconscious of ideas or subjects until written. To convince the understanding, another intelligence dictates when the mind is passive. As the will dictates the movement of the body at rest, involuntarily or naturally it obeys the will, stops when the will commands.

This is carrying the power of another's will over matter one step further, that is, by showing the influence of another's will on your hand, when you yield your will passive. This illustrates the connection between the law of mind and the law of matter, and also the affinity between the material and spiritual worlds, that the unseen influence which is exerted upon the children of men from satanic agencies may be manifest, that they may be delivered from his power. This will give place to a higher mode of communication, recognized in the Word of God, (*i. e.*), speaking to the individual mind, when they learn to listen to the voice of truth. Let the Word of God as already given, be the standard. The Spirit and the Word agree.

This is only the alphabet in the development of the science of spiritual philosophy. As in natural and moral science, so in spiritual science.

Sounds introduced the alphabet, but the writings use the alphabet more intelligibly. The higher developments will occur in their order, as the minds of men are prepared to receive them. No haste will be made to vindicate the standard of truth; though it fall it shall rise again. The chaff will be separated from the wheat, man will learn not to eat chaff, or stop with wonder or amazement to follow outward developments, but look within for the wheat, the bread of life, by investigating the law controlling spiritual life, of which law man's spiritual nature is a subject.

All sciences are progressive in their developments to the understanding of the pupil. Spiritual as well as moral and physical teachings must first be adapted to the capacity of man to receive. The infant first sees and hears, but does not comprehend what it sees and hears. It feels pain, knows not by what law he sees or hears, or feels or tastes or smells, yet he does all this. To him they are facts, and what are facts to one living being, are facts to the whole world; for all God's works are governed by fixed laws, according to the dictates of wisdom. Man's free moral agency is wisely adapted to fixed laws, if obeyed as duty requires. The law of mind is in harmony with man's moral and physical nature. The abuse of this law is attended with consequences the most disastrous to man in time and eternity.

The sickness and suffering of the human family, demonstrate the abuse of physical law. The sin, degradation and wretchedness of mankind, demonstrate the transgression of moral law. The condition of the lost souls in hell demonstrates in characters of living fire, the fatal effects of transgression, to bring to the knowledge of man more fully his high destiny, and the spiritual law to which his spiritual nature is, or should be, a loyal subject. This spiritual Moses or manifestation has been given, and this manifestation is intended to lead man out of spiritual bondage into the liberty of the children of God. The land of Canaan was the land of promise to Abraham, Isaac and Jacob, and to their posterity after them for ever, if they would obey God's commandments, deal justly, love mercy, and walk humbly with God.

In the fullness of time, the bondmen in Egypt sent up a cry for deliverance from the oppression of their enemies, notwithstanding the promise that had been made to their fathers. Had they not cried for deliverance, they would not have been delivered from their enemies. Had not their cry gone up, Moses would not have been sent. Had not Moses been sent, no law or demonstration of the power and mercy of God would have been given at Mt. Sinai, to lead them to the promised inheritance, to the land of their fathers, and to the service and worship of the true God.

Generation succeeding generation, may refuse or accept the covenant of promise, as all are free agents in this particular, and moral agents in doing the will of God. The promised gift of the Father to the primitive church, was the gift of the Holy Ghost to them and their children. The primitive church received this baptism. Their children have wandered long in spiritual Egypt, while some of the true sons and daughters of Abraham, have been weeping between the porch and the altar, for the deliverance of God's people from their sins, and the fulfillment of the new covenant promise above referred to.

The command has gone forth, go ye messengers of light, teaching the way of the Lord more perfectly, that the concealed snares of Satan may be broken, and the captive soul go free from the law of sin and death; teaching that the law in the members, warring against the law of the mind, is self in affinity with Satan; that the law of love in Christ Jesus, destroys this carnal mind or the death of the body of self, while the prayer of faith alone can destroy the power of affinity between the mind that has yielded to evil to obey Satan in the lusts thereof.

Therefore Jesus taught, when ye pray, say, deliver us from evil, which to man is the spirit of Satan in affinity with the spirit of self. This is the carnal mind inherited from Satan, which is at enmity with God, is not subject to his law, neither indeed can be. This is the body of death which the Apostle prayed to be delivered from. He also bore witness, the spirit of life in Christ Jesus shall make me free from the law of sin and death. His servants ye are whom ye obey.

Moses was met by the magicians of Egypt, who wrought many wonders, instigated by Satan to defeat the effect of divine power, to entice Pharaoh to resist the commands of God by Moses, to let the people go into the wilderness to worship their God.

So has Satan met this manifestatien to man, aided by his own servants, by disobedience to the law of God, in calling upon departed friends to communicate to them, through the well-known motive power of spirit upon spirit, of spirit upon matter; making spirits in affinity with evil the channels of error, to spread broadcast upon the earth the doctrines of devils, the doctrines of Antichrist, again reiterating the same subtle devices that Satan did to Eve, thou shalt not surely die.

CHAPTER X.

THE LAW OF NECROMANCY.

You comprehend but in part, what was intended to be taught you, upon the sin of Necromancy. (Allusion to instruction given in missing papers.) We said whoever seeks knowledge from any other source in preference to God, in spirit, it is Necromancy.

This sin is not confined to those who seek knowledge through the spiritual manifestations of this day from the departed of earth. The world is now a self-seeking age, "seeking honor one of another," and knowledge from forbidden sources, as in ages past.

"As it was in the days of Noah, so is it in the days of the Son of Man." All that will heed the truth, will enter the ark. Two of every kind, signifies some of all tribes and nations, tongues and people. As it was in the Jewish church, while they trusted in the law of righteousness, so is it now. The works of benevolence are now substituted for gospel obedience, repentance, charity, faith, by the evangelical churches. The prevailing customs and maxims of a wicked world, have more weight with professedly Christian churches, than the plain truth of God's Word. Few there are who walk by naked faith, as did Noah, rising superior to the opinions of the mass, not giving heed to seducing spirits and doctrines of unbelief, which are to be met with in every man who follows not God, independent of the opinions of his fellow-man, in honesty, sincerity and truth, taking God's Word for his standard instead of the teachings of men, who are reprobate concerning the true life of faith once delivered to the saints.

The men who spied out the promised land of Canaan, through their fearfulness and unbelief, as much seduced the armies of Israel to murmur against God, as the idolatrous nations did afterward. Whoever has an unbelieving spirit, has a seducing spirit, and chills and dampens the faith of the strongest, while within the circle of their influence. The testimony of such is an evil report; these are the dead weights in Zion, the withered branches which must be cut off, the barren fig tree which will be cut down.

Beware how you limit the Holy One of Israel, and say to the inquiring soul, the promise of God is doubtful. Let us not expect too much. Say these in practice and theory; they are to be taken in a restricted sense. Let us not expose ourselves to the ridicule which befell Noah, nor to the dangers of fanatacism, nor undertake without more prospect of success, the conquest of such foes as none have conquered since the disciples' day, nor expect to receive such gifts as were imparted to them. True, say these false teachers, the Bible advocates the doctrine, yet the experience of the Christian world disproves its power to modern believers. "Let God be true, and every man a liar."

In the last days their shall be seducing spirits of unbelief in God's Word.

The channel through which man obtains knowledge from men and books is sanctioned, if the mind rest not in the source or knowledge gained, as an end, making it his God, instead of a means leading to an acquaintance with God.

For this is all the wisest mind can grasp, where intellect is enriched with the combined researches of ages, with the wisdom of the ancients, and the profoundest lore of ancient and modern philosophy. To acquaint the mind with the effect of the laws controlling God's works, is the highest pinnacle which intellectual efforts or pursuits can reach; it is the highest attainment it can make through the intellect to know God.

While the great First Cause of all things is only comprehended through the spirit of faith and love of the affections, and the intuitive powers of the mind, what a high insult to the God of intellect and science, for man to so abuse the author of these gifts, so as to make the unsanctified traditions of the Fathers and the sectarian chain of parties, the rules of his life and practice, building upon the works and theories of the illustrious dead, neglecting and despising at the same time the living oracles of truth, for the deductions of their own vain reasonings.

Divine wisdom alone is the parent tree of all true philosophy. It leads its pupils to fountains of intellectual light, to streams that shall never die, to knowledge that shall never vanish away, to tongues that shall never cease, to prophesies that shall never fail.

While the human intellect that rejects or neglects to draw from these unfailing resources, shall find the knowledge it gains by Necromancy as little enlightening, comforting, sustaining, delivering, as did the first pair in the Garden, when they sought knowledge from a forbidden source, as did Saul, when he inquired of Samuel his destiny, instead of submitting his proud heart to God, and putting away his cherished idols, that God might answer him through the divinely appointed oracles. Knowledge gained without the Divine sanction, is like plucking fruit from the forbidden tree, of which God has said thou shalt not eat; because the fruit is not life, or profitable, or good for the mind. Such knowledge is poisonous to the soul, developed in the hot-bed of self-seeking. Its branches are curiosity and self-reliance; its fruit is presumption, which, gathered in haste, is ripened by other suns than the genial sun of wisdom and experience. The ways of wisdom are tried paths, and bear on their portal gateways the ensign of success. The intellect that enters the paths of truth through these portals of wisdom, is never entangled in the meshes of skepticism and unbelief.

The practical knowledge of gospel truth, which is the fragrance of the tree of science, the nectar in the wine of knowledge, which never intoxicates the limited mind of man, is the knowledge that puffeth not up, behaves itself not unseemly, is not easily provoked, feeleth no ostentation, thinketh no evil. This knowledge is the sun of all the sciences God has given to man. Without this revivifying light to shine upon the page of the human intellect, man is in the sight of God unwise, in spirit an idolator, a worshiper of intellect, a worshiper of the theories of dead men, whom they consult as the standard authors of their favorite sect or party.

The plain letter and spirit of the Divine Oracles are set aside for the most approved and adopted sayings of the Fathers. Their views are sought with zeal by their followers, and are frequently quoted by the disciples of each sect of the age, as of sufficient authority to cause them to reject the plain letter of the Word (*viz.*), the Spirit's teachings in the soul as dangerous, notwithstanding the two witnesses of God, the Old and New Testaments, testify that the true sons of God are led by the Spirit.

The writings of the living and dead, declare it unsafe for the holy man even to follow the teachings of the Spirit in the soul with perfect reliance on the Word, that man may lay hold upon the wisdom and strength of God, in his ignorance and weakness, and obey at any time and at all times acceptably the commands of the law of love. What is this in spirit, but Necromancy? Unsanctified human reason makes out a safer way to guide the soul, to reject what he does not understand intellectually, and what he can not glean from his fellow-man: placing authors upon the pinnacle of wisdom, as the oracles of science and religion, physically, morally, spiritually, as superior to Revelation. This spirit of idolatry and Necromancy, is not confined to the world. The Church of the living God partakes of its sins.

The sin of King Saul was not more reprehensible to God, when he went to the living to consult the holy dead, than now for the living to turn from the commandments delivered unto them, to consult the works of the dead, who, like Samuel, once lived, thus building the tombs of the prophets and garnishing their sepulchers. As their fathers did, "So do ye."

Let not the pure in heart go to the living or dead, to learn the wisdom he lacks, but go to God, who giveth to all men liberally and upbraideth not. Be ye helpers of each other's faith. "Are ye not all brethren?" The consulting of books or minds, whether living or departed, as standard authors, and depending upon them in preference to the spirit of God and his Word, is sinful. The spirit of glorying in the teachings of the wise and learned, is opposed to the spirit of the Gospel, and idolatrous. It inculcates spiritual pride, egotism, sectarian strife in different denominations. This engenders false accusation, evil surmising and whisperings in the camp of the saints.

This self-exaltation and self-emulation among Christian churches, is the bane of witchcraft; having the form of godliness, but denying the power thereof; "Reprobate concerning the faith," yet in practice doing their own works in the name of Jesus, as did the exorcists in the days of the Apostles, and the papal power of Rome since. Let the pure in heart turn away from imitating the practice of such.

Spiritual pride is of the same destroying principle, and is another member of the body of death, that is, the carnal mind. This is exhibited in the practice of some believers, who seek the uppermost seats in the synagogues, and desire to be first in authority; lording it over man's conscience; leaders and guides to the people; self-satisfied, holding up their own experience for the imitation of others, instead of teaching, with St. Paul, that the Spirit has "diversities of operations" and various manifestations, adapted to the circumstances and capacities of minds.

These are blind guides, having plucked one leaf from the tree of life, feel satisfied to rest in the feast of that, and present that to the world as the whole tree, instead of leaving the first principles to go on to higher attainments, not as though they had already attained, "But following on to know the Lord," that they may apprehend that for which they are apprehended of him.

How unwise for such to exalt themselves as leaders, pressing their opinions upon points where the mind is but partially enlightened; censorious, denying to others the rights of conscience. Those are unwise who consider their exercises the only standard of true gospel faith, constraining others to follow them, that they may have whereof to glory as the leaders of a party, examplers of the true faith only in outward works; dictating the manner of life, the manner of dress, the manner of speaking and of preaching, quenching the Spirit — from such turn away.

"Be not many masters, for such fall into condemnation." Let the pure in heart be in the world as was Christ, blameless, who, when he was reviled threatened not; he suffered the contradiction of sinners; he opened not his mouth.

Let the pure in heart be in spirit, among the disciples, as a little child, and servant of all, teachable, esteeming others better than themselves; long-suffering, full of compassion, of tender mercies towards all, even as Christ towards thee: making no difference between the poor and the rich, the wise and ignorant, that ye may be the blameless children of the Most High.

Man's false profession of love for his fellow-man, is rottenness in his bones, when he discovers the absence of the heart's pure love in the acts of his friend: grief drinketh up the spirit. "A wounded spirit who can bear?" God is jealous of the love which is his due from his weakest child, and when he sees this love withheld, he casts his shadow between the injurer and his injured love.

Hypocrisy arms both God and man with abundant cause for withdrawing the confidence of favor from all who practice fraud upon their proffered love. The withdrawing of favor is not revenge; still love your enemy, but wisely deliver yourself from his power, then seek to reclaim him by kind acts of mercy, not confidence. Then shall ye be the children of your Father in heaven, who sends his rains on the just and on the unjust, but only commits his secrets to them that love him. "The secret of the Lord is with them that fear him." "The wicked and his enemies he knoweth afar off."*

* See Appendix, Notes A and B.

CHAPTER XI.

THE LAW OF RECEIVING MANIFESTATIONS BY INTUITION.*

May, 1853.—I. *Ques.* I DESIRE to know how and in what way my mind is now used in the writings, since the transfer of the influence from the hand to the mind, and how it is I write hour after hour upon subjects never before thought of in the light presented?

Could I understand this new process of teaching, of listening to learn instead of studying, I could more passively yield my mind to instruction given, until the whole chain of truths were brought out.

Ans. The reply to your inquiry is, the Spirit of Truth seeks embodiment in such language of thought as your intellect possesses.

The intuitive instead of the perceptive powers of your mind are used. Instruction that comes by intuition, precedes the cultivation of the intellect. This is a power of mind wisely adapted to the wants of ignorant men, who are, from outward circumstances, cut off from such sources of perceptive knowledge as to make them wise unto salvation, or in things necessary for their subsistence and well-being. Because men ordinarily receive knowledge through the outward senses, they overlook the truth

* See Appendix, Note A.

of Revelation, and say instruction to be valid must come through the senses; while either may become the channel of knowledge on various subjects through the Spirit's operations, "Teaching the lips knowledge." Intuitive knowledge is the basis of a sound, independent understanding. It enables men to judge from nature instead of appearances, Solomon like, through the intuitive powers of the soul.

If the understanding is sanctified by perceptive truth and based upon God's Word as a strong foundation, it receives the instruction given from the fountain of Omniscience, and must come through that channel, as all-knowing, speaking like one having authority; yet it takes not mind by force. "He that waits upon the Lord renews his strength."

The Prophet knew this power of mind when he said, "I will hearken and hear what the Lord God will speak unto me." There is in such an understanding a ready response to truth, new or old; it seeks not first to know another's views, saying, "Have the rulers believed on Him?" but this is the language of the honest mind: "We believe not because of thy word, we have heard and seen for ourselves."

When the understanding approves of new truths based upon Scripture, common sense, justice and mercy, these witnesses will carry their convincing testimony into every honest, reflecting heart, to the overthrow of error and tradition and sectarian theology.

Ques. May I here inquire if my mind influences the writing?

Ans. The state of your mind greatly influences it in one respect: your inquiries often interrupt the chain of instruction. When you are perplexed or troubled it prevents the soul from being influenced, and closes the intuitive powers to the voice of Truth. Mind, or the intellect, must listen or be passive to learn from this source, as well as think to learn through the perceptive powers.

Ques. Is there not danger of being wrongly led, through this source?

Ans. Yes, in some respects, great danger; therefore you are taught in the Word to try the spirits by the standard of the Word. The spirits that are not of God reject Christ. In reference to this it is written, "Beloved, believe not every spirit, but try the spirits whether they are of God; because many false prophets are gone out into the world. Hereby know ye the spirit of God: Every spirit that confesseth that Jesus Christ is come in the flesh, is of God." "And every spirit that confesseth not that Jesus Christ is come in the flesh, is not of God; and this is the spirit of Antichrist, whereof ye have heard that it should come, and even already is in the world."

"Ye are of God, little children, and have overcome them; because greater is He that is in you, than he that is in the world."

"They are of the world; therefore speak they of the world, and the world heareth them."

"We are of God; he that knoweth God heareth us. Hereby know we the spirit of truth and the spirit of error."

In these Scriptures quoted, you have a standard for both truth and error. While a probationer you can not be exempt from the assaults of evil spirits. The law of mind and the economy of grace have made provision for resistance and deliverance from evil, but not exemption from the assaults of evil.

This shows you the sources from which good and evil spring, and that there is safety no where but in God. Those who go out to sea without the Word of God, go out without chart or compass, and will as assuredly make shipwreck of their souls, as there are dangers and quicksands in the deep.

Satan deceives such as reject the Word. To destroy the faith of the Gospel, the fires of martyrdom are kindled by the zealous bigot, the self-ruling spirit of Satan, which prefers bloodshed, anarchy and death, to submission, equity and lowliness of spirit.

The spirit that exalts itself above all that is called God, is from beneath, that denies the truth of Revelation, "Teaching for doctrines the commandments of men."

Ques. How can the soul know when it is led by the Spirit?

Ans. The Spirit and the Word agree. "Though an angel from heaven preach any other doctrine than that which is preached, let him be accursed." The Word of God is the only standard and basis of truth in natural and revealed religion. When men reason from physical causes, they are limited to the effects produced from hidden laws in nature; they know not first principles only from analogy. They reason from the effects, then build their theory to correspond to effects. In this manner they deny the record of creation, consequently virtually deny the command to keep the Sabbath day holy. For when they strike out one as false, they must both. The seventh day was as long as the other days named, specified by evening and morning.

Yet men who are shocked at the mutilation and rejection of the Bible by the spiritual skeptic of the day, here bend the truth to their own theory, because the same effects have been produced by the operation of the hidden laws of nature as first originated creation, denying the record of creation as given to be true, that "God spake and it was done, he commanded and it stood fast." So popular is this new theory of men, an unlettered man fears to risk an opinion contrary to that advocated, though it troubles his conscience to give God the lie.

Still further, another theory is raised, reasoning from the effect of what they do understand of matter, denying the resurrection of the body, which is the basis of the atonement. "For if Christ be not risen, ye are yet in your sins," and those that have fallen asleep in Jesus, have perished, that is, resolved back to elementary principles, both soul and body.

If the hope of the resurrection of the body is perished, the hope of immortality and eternal life, which is based upon the resurrection of Christ from the dead, must also perish, for he came to bring life and immortality to light. This Scripture is construed to mean nothing, because human reason sees no wisdom or facts in nature to sustain it.

The third important thing conceded to false philosophy, are truths of the Trinity, as taught in the Word of God, and of the kind and reality of the punishment of the transgressors (*viz.*), the second death, because they look not to the cause or laws in nature which produce the effects described. Thus different parts of Bible truth are conceded as figurative, not real, by different denominations of professing Christians, taking from and adding to, instead of receiving by faith what they can not understand, and obeying from the heart the law of the Lord.

"They heap to themselves teachers having itching ears," who will proclaim their theories according to their standard authors.

CHAPTER XII.

SCRIPTURAL BASIS OF THE ABOVE LAW OF INTUITION.

Ques. I DESIRE to know more of this manner of the mind's operation, that is referred to through the intuitive powers of the mind?

Ans. This development of the hidden law of mind is neither supernatural nor miraculous. It is the natural channel of the Spirit's operations, as much so as hearing or speaking is in accordance with the natural man. If man had never been taught to speak or use the power of his voice, he would be slow to believe this faculty could open up before him such rich sources of enjoyment, and no doubt would excite his unbelief and opposition, quite as much as this new manifestation developing the original law of mind.

Do not regard this as a new development. It is as old as the creation of man, yea, older; it is the basis of intelligence, though so little appreciated.

When the soul waits upon God to be taught, and loves and seeks the truth, there is no promise in his Word more frequently declared, plain, unequivocal and full than this; for example, "Take no thought beforehand what ye shall speak, neither do ye premeditate, but what shall be given you, that speak. For it is not ye that speak, but the Holy Ghost that speaketh in you."

To Moses the Lord said, "Now therefore go, I will be with thy mouth and teach thee what thou shalt say."

Samuel said, "The Spirit of the Lord spake by me, and his word was in my tongue."

"For prophesy came not in old time by the will of man, but holy men of God spake as they were moved upon by the Holy Ghost."

To the disciples it was said, "Take no thought how or what ye shall speak: for it shall be given you in that same hour what ye shall speak. For it is not ye that speak, but the Spirit of your Father which speaketh in you."

"And when they bring you unto the synagogues and unto magistrates and powers, take no thought how or what ye shall answer, or what ye shall say: for the Holy Ghost shall teach you in that same hour what ye ought to say."

"Settle it therefore in your hearts not to meditate beforehand what ye shall answer. For I will give you a mouth and wisdom, which all your adversaries shall not be able to gainsay nor resist."

Again, "They were all filled with the Holy Ghost, and began to speak with other tongues, as the Spirit gave them utterance."

"And it shall come to pass in the last days, saith God, I will pour out my Spirit upon all flesh, and your sons and daughters shall prophesy, your young men shall see visions, your old men dream dreams; and on my servants and on my handmaidens I will pour out of my Spirit in those days, and they shall prophesy."

"He that believeth on Me, as the Scriptures hath said, out of his belly shall flow rivers of living water; but this spake He of the Spirit which they that believe on

Him should receive. For the Holy Ghost was not yet given, because Jesus was not yet glorified."

You see from these quotations, the Spirit that speaks to man the words it shall say without thought or premeditation, is the Spirit of Truth. This manner of teaching is not supernatural, but natural to spiritual life: it is not confined to prophets or apostles, but is promised, is given to all believers, in all ages of the world.

Ques. Some object to the application of this promise to the present time (*viz.*), "And it shall come to pass in the last days (saith God), I will pour out of my Spirit upon all flesh, and your sons and your daughters shall prophesy, and your young men shall see visions, and your old men shall dream dreams; and on my servants and on my handmaidens I will pour out, in those days, of my Spirit, and they shall prophesy." Say they, that was fulfilled eighteen hundred years ago, in the beginning of the gospel dispensation?

Ans. True, that which was spoken of by the prophets, "*began* to be fulfilled," in the last end of the Jewish dispensation; "And if the *beginning* of the gospel dispensation was glorious, how much more shall the *end* be?"

This refers to spiritual blessings. The revelation or manifestation must be through the Holy Spirit to the mind. He is the teacher sent from God. The impression must be made upon the mind and to the mind. God's method of communicating himself to the soul is various.

The infant believer first learns to look and live. Happiness, joy, peace, are the first elements of spiritual life. The believer should not rest here, but should grow in grace and in the knowledge of the truth. Few comparatively look beyond the point of feeling happy; they seek and pray for happiness; if they are happy they feel they have all that is their privilege in this life. Of course, they can not long retain their joy, while happiness instead of holiness is their object of pursuit.

Through the seducing spirit of unbelief they are turned aside unto fables, because weakly and sickly in the faith; and when they should be able to feed others and receive strong meat, they have need that others teach them.

But few walk with God as did Enoch, Abraham, Moses, Samuel, and the prophets. Yet this is just as much the privilege of all Christians as it was theirs, to talk with God in holy communion as a man talks with his friend, if they seek it, as they did.

"With God there is no respecter of persons, but he that feareth him and worketh righteousness is accepted of him."

"Christ hath said all things are yours." But few will listen and believe, saying, "Speak, Lord, for thy servant heareth," notwithstanding the Word of God abounds with such communications from the Lord to the children of men, on temporal, moral, and spiritual subjects, in all ages of the world, before the Christian era as well as since.

If the giving of the letter of His Word, is to take the place of the revelation of himself to the hearts and minds of His people, the Christian dispensation does not exceed in glory the Mosaic. If only in the Word the Lord manifests himself now, the promise of Christ to those that seek him, that he will "manifest himself to them as not unto the world," is without effect.

Again we say, the Word and the Spirit's teachings agree. The Spirit's teachings are based upon the Word.

If the Word had been sufficient for the soul, the Father would not have given the Holy Spirit to instruct the soul into the spirituality of the Word. No man can know God fully from the reading of the Word, "The letter killeth, but the Spirit giveth life."

The Spirit of God alone can reveal God, who is a spirit, to the spirit of man. It is the Spirit that edifieth, and when "the Spirit takes of the things of God and shows them unto the soul," and the soul receives and obeys, then the understanding is illuminated and the soul "built up in the most holy faith."

All law, whether civil or religious, given by God to man, presupposes the ability of man to obey. Law implies protection and penalties. If man is capacitated to obey the law of life, if he is a free moral agent, and as such acts from the volition of his own will, it also presupposes his ability to disobey law, or he could no more justly be the subject of its penalties than a machine, that is, if he only acts as acted upon.

Man then is an accountable being, responsible for the volitions of his will. This capacity to will is from God, and is the image of God in which man was created.

God loves his own moral image (*i. e.*, freedom of choice,) in human nature, and will preserve it in every being, and will only hold man responsible for his acts in proportion to his power and freedom to will.

The penalty of the law falls not upon the man who, contrary to his will, was compelled by a stronger force to act. It rests upon the man who willed the wrong.

In these thoughts, our design is to show you the capacity of every moral human being in securing and rejecting the rewards and penalties attached to the physical, moral and spiritual law controlling his being; consequently showing you the capacity of minds to receive instruction, that the volition of the will determines the source from which man seeks knowledge, either good or evil.

God will ever preserve man's free volition of the affections. Cheerful obedience is the offspring of the will, and is the sweetest incense the soul can offer to his Maker. "Obedience is better than sacrifice, and to hearken than the fat of rams." Here you see hearkening or listening is approved, as well as action; both together complete the offering.

The power of man to close his mind to evil and seek good, proves this; yet the source of this power is from God and freely given to man. Upon this is based man's responsibility in the world and his accountability to God. This instruction will show you the abuse minds are capable of making of Heaven's richest and best gifts to man, including the mysteries of this development of mind.

CHAPTER XIII.

THE LAW OF AFFINITY IN OPERATION.

FURTHER to gratify the oft repeated request for light upon this mysterious subject, we say again, the Spirit of Truth seeks embodiment in such language of thought as your intellect possesses. Your intuitive powers are the channels used. The undeveloped as well as developed natural bent of mind, and style of reasoning, understanding and intellect, are the agents employed by the Spirit of Truth, for the twofold purpose of exemplifying by positive demonstration in your case the law of mind advocated by the manifestation.

The gems of thought this book contains,
Lie scattered in the sand,
That minds like yours may grasp
The truth that purifies the mind.
The style is yours, the truth is not;
To be humble is to be wise;
Truth is the food you seek,
'Tis truth that sanctifies.
Truth is truth in homely garb,
As much as when 'tis clad
In intellect's polished robes.

These teachings are adapted to your range of intellect. The finite mind must first be taught spiritual things by literal figures, little by little.

NOTE EXPLANATORY OF DRAWING THIRD.

The opposite drawing represents the original given in Feb., 1852, when the writer was exceedingly anxious and doubtful as to her duty, or the will of God concerning her in this mysterious manifestation. She was directed to take a sheet of drawing-paper and place her pencil in the center, and make such figures or lines as the hand was moved to make, which should explain to her her future work. This, with a good deal more, was roughly sketched. The figure representing Christ with her in the vessel stilling the storm, was given in the original drawing. When required to give so much of the drawing as is here sketched for this volume, the same was drawn by the influence upon the hand on a much smaller scale, and the figure representing the angel of the covenant, as above delineated, was added. The trumpets here sketched, were first understood to be the silent voice of God in the soul, and no more, not imagining they had any reference to any books that she would write under this influence, from dictation, as she did not commence her journal until months afterwards, and more than a year and a half elapsed before she had any thought of publishing an extract of what she had written.

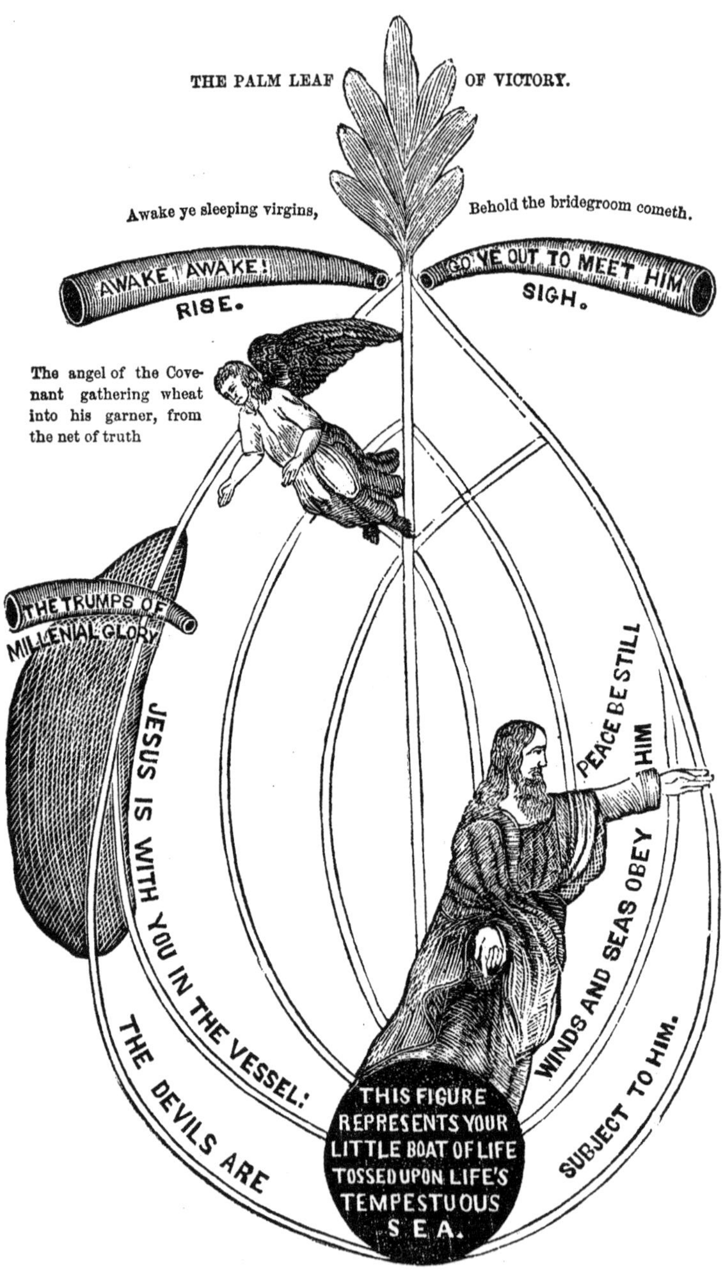

THE PALM LEAF OF VICTORY.
Awake ye sleeping virgins,
Behold the bridegroom cometh.
AWAKE! AWAKE!
RISE.
GO YE OUT TO MEET HIM
SIGH.
The angel of the Covenant gathering wheat into his garner, from the net of truth
THE TRUMPS OF MILLENIAL GLORY
JESUS IS WITH YOU IN THE VESSEL:
PEACE BE STILL
WINDS AND SEAS OBEY HIM
THE DEVILS ARE SUBJECT TO HIM.
THIS FIGURE REPRESENTS YOUR LITTLE BOAT OF LIFE TOSSED UPON LIFE'S TEMPESTUOUS SEA.

Be patient then while you explore,
By faith, these mines of truth.
The one will gain the two, the two
The five, the five the ten.
Thus in due time
Will Christ make you wise, having never learned,
While many wise and learned
Toil all night for naught,
You the net of truth shall let down
At Christ's command, on the right side
Of the ship. Such fishermen are sure to find
And bring safe to land, all it takes.
When the net is truth, it can not break.
The great, the small, truth safely shores
Where error and sin destroy no more.
Thy ship is tossed, by tempest driven
On the boisterous sea of Time,
Yet Jesus pillows his lowly head
On the fore and aft, the front and stern:
Your helsman and your pilot acts,
To steer your ship aright.
He knows the dangers of the deep,
Where the rocks and quicksands lie;
The waves and billows his voice obey,
Nor dare to rise.
His "Peace, be still," is soon obeyed,
The calm succeeds the storm
As light the shade.

How wholesome and healthful to the soul is truth! Your own mind shall be the channel of these divine communings; of being taught essential truths which none can gainsay or resist, if you steadfastly obey the law of mind as brought out to you through the intuitive powers of the soul. Not that your intuition shall be all-knowing, but the channel of communication to other minds from the all-knowing Source of truth.

This gift to minds must be improved like other gifts, to increase its activity and power. This is the way the

Lord designs to lead you and the world in the present so-called spiritual manifestations of the day.

This power of mind is worthy of the effort made to develop it to the world, with the truth that through the affinities of mind good is to be sought and evil repelled. That for this work the mind is capacitated and endowed by the God of nature for the protection, elevation, and sanctification of the noblest powers of man, that he may break the chains of ignorance which fetter the soul, and by the use of his innate powers, go to the Fountain of Truth and draw such supplies of wisdom and grace, as to enable him to overcome the evils which his fallen nature is subject to. Man fell through or by his own perceptive acts, instigated by desire.

Christ redeemed him, brought in forgiveness through the perceptive powers, hearing and believing, which must control the senses afterward. To hide pride from man, he employed the intuitive powers of the mind, for the more direct operation of the spirit.

To satisfy your mind more fully upon this point, that God does instruct his children through the media of the intuitive powers, both sleeping and waking, we will explain what is meant by the prophesy, "Your old men shall dream dreams, &c., and your young men see visions."

The Scriptures teach that the Lord anciently revealed himself to man in the night season, when deep sleep fell upon him, to hide pride from man. This was done through the intuitive powers of his mind, for then his perceptive powers were closed.

The first instance when the Lord caused this deep

sleep to fall upon man, was before he sinned, to show you it was in accordance with the law of mind in a holy state. When he took from Adam the rib of which he made woman, Adam said (when God presented woman to him), "This is now bone of my bone and flesh of my flesh." He knew not this truth, as he knew other things which he learned from his perceptive powers; yet he knew she was made of his bone and flesh, and loved her.

Next we will notice Abram, on whom God caused a deep sleep to fall when watching the covenant offering from being polluted by the fowls, while waiting for the Lord to come as he had promised (now mark, while waiting), he was prepared for the manifestation. And when the sun was going down, a deep sleep from the Lord fell upon Abram, and lo! a horror of great darkness fell upon him. And He said unto Abram in this state (when the outward senses were closed, but the mind listening with overwhelming awe), "Know of a surety that thy seed shall be a stranger in a land that is not theirs, and shall serve them, and they shall afflict them four hundred years.

"And also that nation whom they shall serve will I judge; and afterward they shall come out with great substance, &c."

In that same day, or at that same time, the Lord made a covenant with Abram in a sane state of mind, yet in another way than through the waking perceptive faculties of the body and mind, yet so positively and satisfactorily, that Abram never doubted its source or its truth.

Again, when the Lord revealed himself to Job, it is

written of him, "Now a thing was secretly brought to me, and mine ear received a little thereof. In thoughts from the visions of the night, when deep sleep falleth on man,

"Fear came upon me, and trembling, which made all my bones to shake. Then a spirit passed before my face; the hair of my flesh stood up: It stood still, but I could not discern the form thereof: an image was before mine eyes, there was silence, and I heard a voice, saying, Shall mortal man be more just than God? Shall man be more pure than his Maker.

"Behold, he puts no trust in his servants; and his angels he charged with folly: How much less in them that dwell in houses of clay, whose foundation is in the dust, &c."

This sleep differs from a natural sleep, or a dead sleep (*i. e.*), the sleep of death.

A deep sleep from the Lord fell upon Saul, and by this means he was delivered into the hand of David; that his magnanimous spirit of forgiveness and fear of injuring the Lord's annointed, should teach the heart of the King the wisdom of forbearance.

The Psalmist alludes to this law of mind when he says, "I will bless the Lord who hath given me council, my reins instruct me in the night season. I have set the Lord alway before my face, he is at my right hand, I shall not be moved."

Visions and revelations from God came to the prophets and apostles when in this state of bodily insensibility. Knowledge acquired in this way hides pride from man, because there is no aliment in it for pride to feed upon.

The awe and solemnity attending such visitations,

makes flesh sleep. They fall as dead men to the earth; as said the holy Daniel of himself, "My comeliness is turned to corruption."

The same prophecies which were fulfilled in the last days of the Jewish dispensation, and in the ushering in of the Gospel dispensation, will be again more gloriously fulfilled in the last days of the Gospel dispensation, and the ushering in of the Millennial Glory.

"Then one shall not need to say to another, know ye the Lord, for all shall know him, from the least to the greatest."

When the Lord sends his deep sleep upon man, it is a state of glorious revelations of himself to man; as to Ezekiel, and Isaiah, and Jeremiah.

Again, a discovery of his will concerning individuals and their future course, as to Abraham, and Peter, and Paul, and John the Revelator.

These men were of like passions with others, yet yielding their powers of body and mind entirely to the Lord, they were the honored instruments of good to others. It is the same Spirit, but there are diversities of operations through the intuitive powers as well as through the perceptive. Not making sufficient distinction between the deep sleep which the Lord causes to fall upon man, and natural sleep, men have come to place undue confidence in dreams.

Ques. Are not men more liable to fall into error from the listening attitude of the soul, than through the perceptive faculties?

Ans. No. Said the Prophet, "I will hearken and hear what the Lord God will speak unto me." The "burden of the word of the Lord came unto me," "The Spirit of the Lord rested upon me, &c.," are the frequent expressions of the primitive saints, besides prophets and apostles. Said Christ, "Judge not from appearances, but judge righteous judgment. Judge from nature (*i. e.*), a tree by its fruit. The men of this world often mistake in plain matters of fact, when they judge wholly from appearance.

Satan counterfeits this work of the Spirit, by sudden suggestions and impressions; his work is always soon manifest when operating through the same law of mind. He fills the soul with pride, or perchance false prophesy, self-conceit; saying, ye are the wise men. Yet, Christ says, your wisdom shall die with you, and not profit the soul.

Beware of strong impressions infused in the mind, either good or evil; the conscientious soul is often misled here. The effort of Satan is manifestly to copy the work of the Spirit, to lead the soul into danger, error, fanaticism and presumption; to undertake things impossible for him to perform with profit to himself or others. Many, yea, many, have been urged by Satan into the ministry, who were not qualified by nature, or fitted by grace to do the work of an evangelist, and they have brought a wound and a reproach upon a calling none should engage in but men of clean hands and pure hearts.

No man has clean hands who has an unbelieving heart. To such Jesus hath said, "Why call ye me Lord, and do not the things I say?"

This warning is also applicable to private Christians, who are unprepared to do things and assume responsibilities they are not capacitated for. God always prepares his instruments for the work he calls them to do, if they move in the divine order. The weak things of the world shall confound the mighty, by being made strong. We mean not that men should refuse to act before endowed with supernatural powers. It is by the improvement of what man has, that more is given. We mean he is not required to fill a position in life which requires the ten talents, before he has added two to the one. Such is not in the divine order. The sun rules the day, the moon the night. Learn from nature a divine lesson.

Watch here, turn away from all such sudden impressions of either good or evil, respecting yourself or others. Good influences come not in this way. The Spirit of Truth is the still small voice; you must close your mind to outward things and listen, wait upon God: commune with your own spirit and be still. Resist Satan's powerful impressions to action of any kind, lest you get out of the divine order. He moves the soul from passion, not from principle. The understanding approves not, as the Apostle teaches: the things I approve not, I do. This is Satan's counterfeit of natural intuition.

Yet in avoiding this evil, refuse not to be led by the opposite teaching, which Satan can not copy. When that comes, there is no doubt to the mind; the Spirit of Truth gently takes possession of the meek and quiet mind, while Satan hates such. Here the meek and lowly in heart find rest to the soul, and fill honorably and acceptably the positions designed for them by Providence and grace. Then the Church is edified and built up in the most holy faith. The harvest is great, but the true laborers are few.

It is through the intuitive powers new ideas originate, new mechanical inventions are embodied, both useful and visionary. If acted upon before matured, they prove visionary. This should teach all minds to patiently wait at the same door of Genius, until the scheme or new plan is fully developed. The source from which truth is sought makes a difference, as well as the motive for which it is sought. The best good of mankind and the glory of God, should be the motive in every enterprise, not private gain. Purity of motive is the well-spring of success; genius, of intuition; talent, of intellect; understanding and reason, from both. When new truths are clothed with language, they become subjects of the perceptive faculties to seize upon from within as well as from without, and mature by reflection. The perceptive faculties belong to the intellect, while the intuitive powers belong to the heart and the understanding, the affections or spiritual nature of man. In this sense, too, is man created in the image of his Maker.

The all-knowing God has imparted to man, created in his image, the likeness of all his attributes, which is his moral image (*i. e.*), as the shadow is to the substance. Contrast the resemblance—the intuition to the Omniscient, the finite to the Infinite, the present to the Omnipresent, the mighty to the Almighty, the mortal to the Immortal, reproduction to creation.

The creature man, when holy, is a miniature likeness of his Maker. When all his powers, physical, mental and spiritual, are fully and perfectly developed, as they are capable of being in the present life, how godlike may man become. The mastery of one or more powers of the soul, distinguishes him among his fellow-men; and his influence, through the perfection of that one or more developed quality or gift of nature, bears him on irresistibly, like a mighty torrent, over the opposing obstacles to his destined greatness, and he stands before the world a ruler, a conqueror, the molder of minds and destinies of men yet unborn, through the influence of his godlike greatness.

Were all minds bent on the development of their natural powers for this praiseworthy object, for the good of the whole, how many new channels would be open for the spread of truth, and health, and happiness to mankind.

But alas! alas! self is the nucleus around which the noblest powers of men are made to cluster. What will not bring fame, or power, or wealth to self, is unworthy of effort to such. In this sickly atmosphere, the godlike gifts of men are undeveloped, stinted, capricious, exhibiting the meteor-like glare in the moral heavens for a time, then setting in darkness, which leaves the moral world in greater darkness for its disproportioned unsteady glare of light for a day. When such lights become darkness, how great is that darkness. Yet in every soul of man there lies such powers. If still buried and undeveloped, it is through his neglect or the neglect of others. If lighted by the fire of genius and truth, they will glow as luminaries in the moral heavens, to brighten the pathway of every traveler they meet. If devoted to sin and selfishness, these meteor lights set in the pestiferous atmosphere of death and darkness, a prey themselves to vice, degradation and death.

The operations of the mind are comparatively little studied by the scientific. Its influence upon matter is mighty, in both locating and repelling disease. A diseased mind can induce real disease in the physical man;

so by a strong concentrated effort of the will, have the absorbents been stimulated to take up and throw off disease. Local disease, before it becomes organic, may be dislodged, if the mind of the patient is healthy and the effort continued judiciously for a time. More can be done by the patient than by the physician thus to overcome disease.

Ques. How can disease be induced by the mind?

Ans. Through the morbid fearful condition of the mind, the effort nature always makes to resist and throw off disease is checked, and inflammation is located where the mind is fearful there is or will be disease. This fear weakens the powers of nature, which now need the stimulus of the will to resist and repel disease, to protect the weakest organs.

The influence of mind upon matter, is manifest in ways which even the scientific consider impossible, but which is produced by the simplest process of nature. For instance, thoughts penned upon paper by a strong mind are independent, ruling influential intellect, when placed upon the seat of the affections, brain or forehead of another person of similar yet more delicate organization of mind; the spiritual influence of thought imparted to the material (which is matter) impresses the mind. When placed upon the head, the perceptive faculties can not grasp it without the medium of the senses; yet they are so affected by the influence as to produce the peculiar sensations that are realized upon the nervous system. Then when carried to the seat of the affections, which is the outlet, so to speak, of the intuitive powers of the soul, the brain is influenced through the intuitive powers of the mind, which is the only channel for the operation of this influence, an enthusiasm is felt like inspiration, a strength or vigor of mind before unknown; by this increase of spiritual influence, imparted first to the letters from the powerful mind in affinity with its more delicately organized counterpart, in the individual who speaks under the influence of the inspiration of the natural thoughts and sentiments and spirit of the absent writer.

This is as true of the power of the mind, through the channel of other substances, to impress both the perceptive and intuitive powers, as it is true that the mind can be moved by the power of eloquence or argument. Holy men are aided by the indwelling spirit in the Word they study, to speak as by inspiration, with power in the Holy Ghost. It is what the Apostle meant by praying in the spirit and with the understanding, and singing with the spirit and with the understanding. They partake by study the spirit of the inditer — "Thy words are spirit and life." The secret power of those distinguished for oratory, for eloquence, and for vocal musical powers, lies in the fact that the intuitive gifts of the mind are superior to the perceptive powers, yet they know not by what law of mind they thus excel their neighbor.

What is conceded to them as a special gift, is only the improvement of a natural gift. The intuitive taking the lead of the perceptive powers, they speak and sing from natural science. These individuals act from nature, instead of imitating artificial life, and are called natural speakers and natural singers, simply because nature's laws are obeyed.

All men love to listen to native eloquence; it allies

the being to angels and God. These make no effort of the intellect to please, but remain in that sense passive. For the intuitive powers, which they have learned to trust to, speak through them. Such always speak, pray and sing with effect and power, which no art can imitate.

We do not mean to be understood, if all acted from nature, all would be alike gifted. The intuitive, as well as the perceptive powers of the mind vary. Yet if all would study to know themselves by nature's standard, instead of measuring themselves by artificial codes, they would be wiser, happier and better men. Men are endowed by nature with such gifts (if improved) to just fit them for the position in life God designed them to fill, for the best good of the whole. Therefore, man should not "Reply against God, saying, Why hast thou made me thus?" for the potter has power over the clay, to make one vessel to honor and another to dishonor; or in other words, hath the right and power to qualify one to fill honorable, responsible stations, to bear the burdens of kingdoms, and countries, and communities, living wholly for others, in the midst of hosannas and reproaches, to poise the balance between pride and power, while another is called to enjoy the quiet of home associations in an humbler sphere. Yet both may be equally dear to God, each filling the position he is adapted to for the best good of society; not as peculiar favorites of Heaven, but as important to the service and the well-being of community as a whole.

Ques. Can all minds, by their writing, produce the effect above referred to on other minds?

Ans. No. It is the man who acts from nature that

possesses this power, and no other; and he in proportion as he does so act

Both the superficial and artificial love native eloquence, simplicity, innocency and purity in others, and bow to this intuitive power of the soul, even in the savage, as angelic and godlike, with reverence. This you know from observation. Such men and women, who act from nature, possess a majesty, a commanding influence, which artificial acquirements, dress and beauty can never win. The one is in proportion to the other. The sluggard, though scientific, who neither acts nor thinks independently, casts into a deep sleep by his listless, dormant influence. He is felt, but the listener will sleep too, in spite of his efforts to awake.

Such listless speakers are a curse to communities. Thus the Lord said, "I would ye were either cold or hot, but because ye are lukewarm, I will spew thee out of my mouth."

To illustrate still further this influence of mind: No individual can carry about his person a written letter from a ruling mind superior to his own, without feeling more or less of its influence. If he knows it to be the production of a genius, or a military chieftain, it will inspire thoughts and feelings in unison with what they do know of his or their characters; while if he know it to be a rebellious, seducing, unbelieving spirit, opposed to right, it will impart its own spirit. The sooner he parts with the latter the better.

Man has no right, when he knows the effect of evil, to cherish it. The written as well as the spoken words of a holy, independent, self-possessed pioneer in truth, will exert a powerful influence over the wavering, fickle, unstable soul, trying to walk in the same path. While he cherishes the spirit of the letter in his possession, or feels the power of his words, he will not be likely to perform a mean, a sinful act. This can not be otherwise. So you may carry out the influence of mind upon matter.

The holy men of God anciently were so imbued with the Divine spirit in their close walk with God, that the Prophet's staff, the rod of a Moses, the garments from the persons of the Apostles, wrought mighty wonders; this was in accordance with the law between mind and matter. Faith operating through this law was its agent. "Can a man take fire into his bosom and not be burned?" Can he mingle in evil society and not be corrupted? Can he tamper with sin and unbelief, smile and greet it in the market-places, in the synagogues and streets, in the uppermost seats, and not be harmed by it? No. In all these many ways, come out from the evil in the world, and be separate; touch not, taste not, handle not, lest ye be defiled thereby, and ye shall be my sons and daughters, saith the Lord Almighty.

This secret power of mind, between friends in sympathy, who possess equal powers of intellect, and are adapted by the natural qualities of the heart to become friends, can test this fact by this hidden law of mind.

The weakest physical organization will be the most susceptible to the influence. Yet the strong physical man will feel the influence of another mind, his equal, or counterpart, in the other sex; the impression will be agreeable to him, soul-elevating, cheering, in unison with his own longing affinities for a mind in unison with himself. This law of affinities in its various manifestations, is the basis of friendships, such as God designed when he created them male and female and blessed them as one. Let such as seek friends, seek them through nature's laws; perfect affinities sometimes meet. Yet artificial society is a great barrier to true estimates of character, as well as a barrier to the developments of mind, that makes the soul happy.

If men would reverse the order of education, cultivate the heart, and develop the natural powers of infant minds, then train them intellectually for what nature capacitates, always keeping in check impulse, strengthening and developing principle, nipping in the bud the exacting spirit that self acquires by indulgence, in this way the mind would soon become vigorous, elastic, bending to circumstances and necessities with principle, thus qualified by nature and grace to act the part assigned to each by God.

Why should you think any of this overdrawn, when you know from observation, and the power of your own mind that you can discern positive and repelling influences, when a word has not been spoken, or a look exchanged?

Have you never felt an unhappy, depressing influence in the presence of another, whose life and acts you were a stranger to?

Again, when you first saw a stranger, you felt the power of his character, as beaming out in his countenance, before you heard his voice or fame. This secret hidden law reveals the truth. The spirit of the man is impressed on his features and upon all minds and matter surrounding him, imparting life or death.

If men would read character in this way, and know their characters were to be read by men from nature's book here, as well as in yonder space, they would be less willing to exert any evil influence and expose their criminal deficiencies, by seeking to be first or known in the assembly of the people, until prepared to edify; "The spirit edifieth, the letter, without the spirit, killeth." Such men as have no life in them are the weights in Zion, they are the cumberers of the ground.

Ask the man of God, who feels the power of the Spirit, and has been taught thereby to discern the influence of mind upon mind in his congregation, and has watched the effect of his own spirit upon others, and felt the reacting influence of their minds upon himself, when the truths he uttered were rejected by individuals so powerfully as to close his mouth, he being alone, and he would say, I can do nothing here, where unbelief and error prevail. At this juncture one lone individual would enter the church, with his soul beaming with the power and unction of the Spirit. The speaker's soul, in unison with that mind, would catch the flame, while the other sat silently unconscious of the power his presence was exerting among the people and upon the speaker. By this reinforcement of spiritual life, the speaker rallies; this raises the flame of union and sympathy between them still higher, until both hearts overflow. The congregation feel now their skepticism is taken by force, they know not why. They could resist words of wisdom from one alone, now a chain unseen encompasses them, there is power in words. Light breaks the spell of darkness, the sinner melts and yields his opposition, unbelief flies, victory turns on Zion's side, God is honored, souls are saved.

This is all produced from the powerful influence of mind in agreement, of mind upon matter, as well as mind upon mind. This is called influence, or the power of association. The face and appearance is an index of the mind.

When Moses became faint from opposing influence, Aaron and Hur held up his hands, then the Israelites prevailed; when they ceased to do so, the Amelekites prevailed.

Learn from this the power of a holy life, and go forth strengthening the weak hands and lifting up the weak in faith, through the intuitive powers of the Spirit. So seek to be imbued with the true spirit of life, as to unconsciously change by your presence the atmosphere of skepticism and hatred to love and purity, holiness and faith.

Ques. Can minds in this age of the world, be so under the influence of Divine Grace, as to be able to do those mighty works which the apostles did?

Ans. "Greater works than these shall ye do, said Jesus, because I go to my Father. Hitherto have ye asked nothing in my name: ask, and ye shall receive, that your joy may be full."

The soul imbued with the Spirit of God, can do all things God wishes him to do; all things are possible to such a soul. The mind of the infinite Jehovah is universal, and covers every range and grade of intellect, and is not limited by means or power of adaptation, to time, place and circumstances. With him there is no respecter of persons. The same works in kind may not be necessary to be wrought now as anciently. There may be no wonders necessary to be wrought to convince a cruel king; no Red Sea necessary to be divided, no rock necessary to be smitten to give the people drink; yet the power of God is not limited, it may work in many other ways equally glorious, suited to times and emergencies.

How unwise to let go the strong arm of the Lord to work in and through the soul, because there are no lepers to be cleansed in Israel, no battles to be fought in Canaan, no bitter waters in the wilderness to be made sweet, no altars of Baal to be consumed with literal fire from heaven. Yet these men who wrought these wonders through faith, were men of like passions with others. Seek not to perform the same acts as tests of the Divine power; these acts served the day and circumstances in which patriarchs, prophets and apostles lived; the work of each differed. So Jesus said to such as should believe on him, "Greater works than these shall ye do, because I go to my Father." The presence of a holy man is a check to vice and folly. The example of a holy man may lead multitudes from the red sea of sin into the promised land of rest, as really as did Moses. His staff or his garment may not raise one sick or dying sinner, but the influence of faith, properly exerted, may save multitudes from want and extravagance, from the prison and gallows, and lastly from hell.

Expect this grace in the way God has appointed for each to labor, expect all you need, as you need it, and when you need it. Fear not, it is your Father's good pleasure to give you the kingdom. Be bold, be strong; the Lord loveth the valiant in heart.

The intuitive power is the channel for the development of the natural abilities, and makes man an independent character, while the perceptive faculties are the channel for the intellect. There is a distinction between natural and acquired abilities. Such men as overlook the first and rely upon the last, never act from nature, nor feel from nature, nor listen to the voice of life within.

They are all outward, artificial, they live upon excitement, upon public opinion, taking the fashionable or intellectual world for their guides; they think, do, act and live, as others do, they have no moral power to resist the popular tide to evil; to do otherwise than the world they worship, would be to them annihilation.

These minds may be called intellectually great, because scientific; but neglecting to cultivate the natural heart, through the intuitive powers of the soul, they fail to adapt themselves to the realities of life in nature, which requires matter-of-fact knowledge of the heart, to give and receive true happiness. Nature is her own teacher; she heeds not the pride of superiority in her pupils, she deals out her treasures of love with an unsparing hand to all who look to her as the well-spring of life, and rewards the diligent seeker for wisdom with treasures untold.

The man who cultivates both heart and intellect as a source of good to others, and usefulness and happiness to himself, is the godlike man, and will reap what he has sown; while others neither feel intuitively nor perceptively, for "The spirit of sloth killeth." Others are dead in trespasses and sins. These heed not the wail of woe sounding continually in their ears. "These are without natural affection, truce breakers." Those controlled by the pure deep affections of the heart, are most susceptible to the influences of nature.

The effect above alluded to, can only be produced upon persons of like sympathies and like affinities, of most delicate and refined organization, when the mental and moral faculties predominate over the animal, and the intuitive over the perceptive.

You will know more of this hidden power of the spiritual law of mind hereafter, with other hidden springs which are beginning to flow and to elicit the attention and inquiry of scientific minds on both continents.

Ques. Can printed documents produce the same effect as written?

Ans. No. It is the spirit in the written words, imparted by the writer to the paper by the motive power of spirit. "As in water face answereth to face, so is the heart of man to man."

Printed documents possess a power which reaches the soul, but not like the manuscript or words of the friend; the one moves the heart, the other dwells in it. Said the Psalmist, "O! how love I thy law! I have hid thy word in my heart."

When the sentiments of friends on all points find a lodgment in the heart of each, then the two are agreed to walk together, as Enoch walked with God. This alone is union, or agreement. There can be no union in evil. Men may join hand in hand to do evil, yet there is no union, nor reliance to be placed in such. The traitor to his God will, if his selfish interest require, be a traitor to his best friend and country. Evil is the opposite of union. Union is the imperishable fruit of holiness, and such union brings blessings and agreement. Two can not prevail with God, according to the promise, to receive whatsoever they ask, unless they are agreed as touching the thing they desire. God is not mocked, he knows the power of union of souls in faith. For this union Jesus prayed, "I will, Father, that they may be one, even as I in thee, and thou in me, that they may be one in us."

It is the privilege of believers to be thus united, but

where do you find them? "Out of the same mouth proceedeth blessing and cursing. These things ought not so to be." Think not the lips that breathe a curse, or bitter word against one, can bring a blessing upon another. Yea, bless and curse not, think no evil, give no place to the devil. If prayer is not prevailing, look to the cause; there was not agreement. The hand of the Lord is not shortened, that it can not save, nor his ear heavy, that it can not hear. Could this law of mind be properly estimated, it would work a moral revolution in the hearts of the partially saved. Thus, you see, to walk with God, to prevail in prayer, to be led by the Spirit, and to be one in affinity, there must be a perfect union of faith and love between man and God.

CHAPTER XIV.*

THE HOLY SPIRIT THE TEACHER OF EARTH AND HEAVEN.

Ques. How may I know that the angels are taught by the Holy Spirit, as the Scriptures are silent upon the subject?

Ans. Learn this: Angels are not self-wise. The Holy Spirit is their teacher, therefore, that the family of earth and heaven might be one. Thus hath God sent his Holy Spirit into the world, to be the inspirer of truth in every man's heart that cometh into the world.

God is the source of all good. The Spirit proceedeth forth from the Father, and is the divine essence of truth. Whatever the Spirit of Truth teacheth, is in harmony with the past revelations God has made in his works and Word. Whether man or angel be the messenger of truth, him receive, but not to doubtful disputation.

The angels are taught by symbols or figures, as well as intuitively; for how can a created mind comprehend the Infinite?

"He maketh his angels spirits, and his ministers a flame of fire." Who are his ministers but the seven lamps of fire, which proceedeth out of the throne, which

* The questions given at the beginning of this chapter, relate to certain chapters which were lost after they had been written out.

are the seven spirits of God, commissioned to burn before the throne day and night?

Who are the four beasts full of eyes behind and before, having six wings full of eyes?

Who are the four-and-twenty Elders falling down before the throne, when the beasts cry, Holy, holy, to Him that sitteth upon the throne, and the Lamb, for ever and ever?

Why this representation to the angels which John saw, but to teach them the plan of salvation, by which man was redeemed, which the angels desired to look into?

The seven spirits of God, represent, first, the word of his power manifest in creation. Second, the gift of his Son in man's redemption. Third, the gift of the Spirit, which manifests itself in prophesy, and in the inspiration of the Word. Fourth, the gift of the Gospel, good news and glad-tidings. Fifth, the gift of repentance. Sixth, the gift of faith. Seventh, the gift of the Holy Ghost, the baptism into the nature of Christ, by the soul's drinking of Christ's cup of suffering, in dying to self and the flesh, as Christ did, also to rise with him in newness of life, as Christ rose from the dead.

Ques. May I inquire here, what is the difference between the third and seventh named?

Ans. The first is the eternal Spirit of Truth and Light, proceeding from the Father, before being associated in his mission with human nature.

The Divinity of the life of truth, associated with humanity, is the Holy Ghost, which sanctifies and saves to the uttermost from self and sin.

These are ministers of God in man's redemption, which angels behold before the throne. They proceed out from the throne, because they show the angels they are from God, and signify his good-will to man.

The four beasts are also symbols, representing the four kingdoms which are to stand upon the earth, before the setting up of the fifth kingdom, which is to unite all the kingdoms of earth of the saved into one glorious kingdom, over whom Christ is to reign King of nations, as now King of saints.

The four-and-twenty Elders represent the dynasties of earth, out of which the universal church was gathered, which fall down before the throne, worshiping Him that sat upon the throne, casting their crowns before Him, saying, "Thou art worthy, O Lord, to receive glory, honor, and praise."

This has been given you to show you through what mediums the great God communicates himself to angel and man, that they may learn by symbols to comprehend of his nature what they could never otherwise learn of Him. This knowledge comes to both by intuition and perception.

How reasonable, then, man should open his mind to truth, when communicated through the media of spirit upon spirit, or by angel, or by the direct teachings of the Holy Spirit, which is no fable, as some would make you think.

God is truth. The Holy Spirit is the teacher sent from God. Learn of Jesus to be meek and lowly in spirit, and you shall find rest to the soul.

God promised to give his angels as ministering spirits to the world, and he has. They encamp about the just, they do the will of God in heaven, as you should on earth, in love. Angels are all taught of God, therefore what they communicate is pure. Those streams are not infected with self or worldly policy. "The wisdom of the world is foolishness with God." The turbid channels of instruction are only from earth and hell.

For years your mind has been held to this subject. Others, beside those who write as you do, have been conscious of angelic influence. What you receive from good angels belongs not to the angels, but to God; therefore in all things make your request known unto God, and what you receive take as from Him in love, giving God thanks.

Do you not see the chain that is let down to earth from God the Father to vile man? First, the spirit of prophesy, then his Son, then the Holy Ghost, then his angels and ministers of burning lamps of fire before the throne, which are continually doing the bidding of God, day and night, in both worlds. Did man on earth possess more gratitude for his blessings, he would be happier and more like the saved in heaven.

Seek to have your own heart touched by these ministers of fire, as with a live coal from off the altar where they minister continually. The seven spirits of God go out into the earth for man's perfect salvation.

All these gifts are yours, as well as the leaves of the tree of Life; which tree grows on either side of the river, and the leaves of the tree are for the healing of the nations.

They that overcome shall walk with me in white (*viz.*), in innocency, purity, faith, and loving trust.

Ques. What are the leaves of the tree on this side of the river?

Ans. The words of promise in the written Word.

CHAPTER XV.

THE LAW OF SPIRITUAL INFLUENCE.

Ques. On what principle are the so-called "spiritual rappings" to be explained?

Ans. It is the influence or effect of breath upon air. The senses are to the perceptions what the mind is to the spirit. The bodily senses are the mediums of instruction to the mind. Therefore Jesus taught, "Faith comes by hearing, and hearing by the *Word* of God." "The *Word* was made flesh and dwelt among us." Organic life uniting with vaporous matter to form all substances, filling all space, is the vitality of the elements in nature upon which light, air and sound are based.

Organic life is also a constituent of spirit, breath, and matter, and powerful in its effects in nature. The breath of spirit, like the breath of man upon air, will cause vibration, which produces sound, according to fixed law, adapted to the organism of the hearing ear.

Hearing is the channel or medium of faith to the mind or intellect, according to revelation. Sound is to the ear, what breath is to the body. "One can not say to the other, I have no need of thee." The breath of man upon material substances produces sound. The organs of speech articulate sounds. This is illustrated by the breath on the instrument, or the sound of the voice upon air, causing the air to vibrate, producing musical sounds, or discordant sounds, according to the will of the performer.

The manifestations of sound are controlled by fixed laws and adapted to the moral agency of all spirit, and the organism of all flesh, and is a channel of wisdom to the soul.

Therefore man is accountable for the use he makes of this law. "For every vain and idle word that man shall speak, he shall give an account thereof in the day of judgment."

Since the bodily senses are the avenues to the soul from objects without, how important that these senses should be under the control of sanctified reason.

Faith comes by hearing, so does unbelief; hearing is the result of sound. This law, then, if abused, produces evil, while if obeyed, it is the power of God to the saving of the soul.

These hints are to show you the adaptation of nature's law to the senses of the body, and are also wisely adapted to man's free moral agency. That in every respect, physically, morally and spiritually, man is a subject of nature's laws, and as such is accountable how he hears, how he speaks, how he sees, how he feels.

The dumb can not speak, the deaf can not hear, nor the blind see; consequently the only outward mediums left for knowledge to such, are feeling, tasting, smelling. Causes which cut off these channels to the soul, prevent the development of mind here, as the amputation of the limb prevents the activity and usefulness of the body. The consequence is, he is taught by intuition to obey the appetites, to taste, feel and smell.

These sensations are instrutced by intuition to desire knowledge. Knowledge of objects calls out love, helplessness teaches dependence, inspires hope, seeks mercy, and mercy saves.

These physical deformities are the result of abused law, the effect of moral evil.

For such, and all that class of unfortunate human beings who suffer from like causes, independent of their volition, ample provisions are made through the atonement. When mind leaves the body, it commences its true physical, and moral, and spiritual training, so to speak (*i. e.*), the mind only suffers a temporary loss from the sins of others.

Thus you see Christ is to man a whole Saviour. The resurrection and the life.

"He that believeth on me," said Jesus, "though he were dead, yet shall he live."

Ques. What am I to understand by the physical training commencing when the soul leaves the body of the idiot or deformed?

Ans. There is a spiritual body in every human organism, yet it hears not outwardly, when the physical senses are closed. When first disembodied, it is the same ignorant mind it was in the body. The fullness of the atonement makes provision to repair the evils of sin in every form; then and there it must begin to learn truths which are conveyed to infant minds here through the medium of the physical senses. The spiritual body sees, hears, feels, tastes, smells, as well as the physical body, when separated from it. This is the medium of spiritual training preparatory to the resurrection of the mortal body, which will be adapted again to the spiritual body, or soul. As spirit gives form to matter when nature's laws are obeyed in its embryo state, so will it in the resurrection state.

It is sown in corruption, it is raised in incorruption. Do you not see from this, that provisions are made for the development and perfection of the natural body? Then it shall be like the spiritual life, or adapted to it, being clothed with immortality. Not like the deformed body that was first the home of the spirit, which was made what it was by the disobedience of another. "As in Adam all die, so in Christ shall all be made alive."

The mortal puts on immortality at the resurrection of the just. The resurrection body must exceed in glory the appearance of the spiritual body, or soul, before the resurrection. Humanity was associated with the divinity of Christ. He became the first fruits of them that slept, he honored humanity and triumphed over death. Man will be raised in the likeness of his resurrection body. The glorified exceeds in beauty the resurrection body. We shall be satisfied, said the Psalmist, when we awake in his likeness, "for we shall see him as he is." This glorified or transfigured body, refers not to his resurrection body, but to the glory which he had with the Father before the world was, in whose image man was first created, when glorified man will not only bear his image, but be like him, for he shall see him as he is. "Eye hath not seen, nor ear heard, neither hath it entered into the heart of man to conceive, the glory which he hath prepared for them that love him."

Created beings are not by nature either infinite or immortal, but may be clothed upon with immortality, by

Him who only hath immortality to bestow, who dwelleth in light unapproachable.

Man is a dying creature, without eternal life. Man is mortal until clothed upon with immortality. How high is the destiny of the redeemed of earth.

O think of his restoration, not only to what man was before he fell, but to be made like the Son, heirs, and kings, and priests unto God, until your heart expands with the hope of eternal life! Perfected physically (*i. e.*), the body, as well as mentally and spiritually, at the resurrection morn.

For your further edification, we will illustrate from Scripture the effect of the motive power of the breath of God in creating spirit and matter, that you may not think it strange that spirits, which were once created in the image of God, should produce the effects attributed to unseen agencies, by the power they possess. By the word of the Lord were the heavens made, and all the hosts of them by the breath of his mouth.

"For he spake and it was done, he commanded, and it stood fast."

"By the breath of God frost is given, and the breadth of waters is straitened."

"The Lord God breathed into man the breath of life, and he became a living soul."

"Christ breathed upon his disciples, saying, Receive ye the Holy Ghost."

"Then said he unto me, Prophesy, Son of man, come from the four winds, O breath, and breathe upon these slain, that they may live."

"So I prophesied as the Lord commanded, and the

breath came into them, and they lived and stood up an exceeding great army."

"And he shall smite the earth with the rod of his mouth; and with the breath of his lips shall he slay the wicked."

Here you see the motive power of breath in giving natural and spiritual life, and resurrection from death. By the word of this power worlds were created, and all the hosts of them.

As the Father hath life in himself, so hath he given to the Son to have life in himself; therefore he said "I have power to lay down my life (give up my breath), I have power to take it again, for this power have I received of the Father."

And as the Father gave the Son to have life in himself, so hath the Son given to the believer power to have life in him — that ye may be one, even as the Father and Son are one. This breath is to spiritual life, what heat is to animal life. This the soul lost by sin. Christ alone can restore this breath of life to man, and while man by faith retains it, he lives in Christ, and no longer. There is great beauty and force in this truth, if the mind can grasp it without prejudice. It shows the connecting link between the creature and the Creator, and the unity existing between the Creator and all created things (*i. e.*), before sin entered the world.

The effect of sin upon the spirit is hardening, stupefying, retrograding, heathenizing, while the penalty is death. Its breath is putrid, blasting the fairest bud of hope. Its vitality is sustained by the noxious fluids of unbelief, hatred, malice, guile, evil speaking, evil surmising, variance, and all kindred vices.

Unbelief is the most deadly poison which infects the mind of man. It is the vital breath of hell. Beware how you cherish or breathe in the seducing spirit of unbelief. Listen not to temptations from the world, the flesh, and the powers of darkness. Say to all as Christ did to Satan, "Get thee behind me."

June 3, 1853. On various occasions we have introduced the subject of the laws of nature (of sounds in particular), as a medium of spiritual intercourse between God and man, between angel and man, angel and angel, Satan and angels, Satan and man. As in human science, so in spiritual. Sounds introduced the alphabet, writing used the alphabet more intelligibly.

"He that formed the eye, shall he not see? and the ear, shall he not hear?"

The soul has its spiritual senses and is governed by the same laws as the bodily senses; for the organism of mind or spiritual perceptions, is adapted to the laws of nature, the same as the physical senses.

By the same law of sound did the sons of light rejoice and sing together at the creation of man. They announced the birth of creation and the birth and resurrection of Christ to mortal ears.

The trump of God was heard by man at the giving of the law at Mt. Sinai. Again will it be heard at the resurrection morn, when man is summoned to give an account how he has kept that law.

The voice of God was heard by mortal ear at the baptism of Jesus Christ. And they heard a voice, saying, "This is my beloved Son in whom I am well pleased." Nature's laws are the channels of the Spirit's operation through the senses. Hearing is based upon sound, vision upon light, while the human breath is dependent upon air.

There are other instances where the patriarchs and prophets talked with God and angels. This was in accordance with nature's laws, not contrary to them. Holy beings never violate a law of nature, nor counteract it, nor act contrary to it.

As spirit is above matter, and God above nature, so the special providences of grace can supersede nature's laws to bring in life out of death. In this way are the believing saved, the sick healed, the dead raised; not contrary to nature, but above and beyond nature, in accordance with the higher spiritual law of life.

Angels are the ministers of His new covenant of mercy, delegated with the power of special intervention, in answer to prayer, to supersede general or fixed laws of nature, to save and deliver from danger and death (by the power of faith), such as trust in God.

These elements of nature are among the agents employed by God to save the world, and act as the agents of God in recording the deeds of the just and the unjust upon the eternal page of truth, and also will be the agents employed to execute the penalty of death upon the transgressor of holy law, as well as form the abode of the eternal, who dwelleth in light unapproachable.

CHAPTER XVI.

NATURE, AS THE AGENT OF LIFE AND DEATH TO THE SOUL.

Ques. How can it be that the elements of nature are employed in the opposite works of recording man's acts, of executing the penalty of death, and forming the abodes of light?

Ans. Faith comes by hearing, hearing by the Word of God. He formed man with bodily organs of speech, adapted to the law of sound and the intelligence of mind through the media of the senses, through which God designed man to seek knowledge and life.

Every sound or voice has its signification. The croaking frog, the chattering bird, the lowing beast, the barking dog; yet to man these are unintelligible. He knows not what is piped or harped by these uncertain sounds. Yet these are also produced by the same law adapted to the instincts of the brute creation, as the words of wisdom spoken with the understanding is adapted to the capacity of mind and the hearing ear.

This law is subject to abuse, the same as all law, and visits its own penalty upon the transgressor. When perverted, it becomes a broad channel to evil, and like other perverted gifts, finds the sinner out. For words spoken in secret shall be proclaimed upon the housetop.

How, do you inquire, is this to be done? By the tale-bearer that reveals secrets?

No. By these elements in nature, which convey every thought, word, and whisper to its destined place, more truthfully than the telegraphic wire conveys its communications by the motive power of machinery and electrity. "For every word that man shall speak, he shall give an accouut thereof in the day of judgment."

This is done with all the philosophy of science in nature, operating silently, unseen and unknown to man, as the other laws of nature operate, which are only known by their effects in nature; as, for instance, gravitation and the growth of vegetation. The partial effect of these hidden yet active laws, is in all men. Yet understand that the power and varied uses of light, air and sound, are but partially known or appreciated, as the agents of God in the elevation of fallen man, which contributes so largely to his happiness, physically, morally and spiritually. Words fitly spoken, how good they are. "They are like apples of gold in pictures of silver."

The song of praise, how sweet is it, both on earth and in heaven; united with angelic harps above, and musical instruments which are the delights of men on earth.

What rich sources of enjoyment are furnished for men and angels, based upon the laws of nature. These common gifts of God men use, without considering their right use brings happiness, and their abuse, sorrow. Because the law of sound is adapted to man's nature, he has no right to corrupt minds by evil communications; no right to use it as a channel of consulting with familiar spirits contrary to God's Word, because the act is possible, which fact minds must admit is possible, or God would never have prohibited it. Let the dead (*i. e.*), such as are dead in trespasses and sins, bury their dead, but follow thou me, said Jesus; inasmuch as if he had said, no more worship friends, or look to them as your oracle, but worship God.

Let nothing hinder the soul from following Jesus, from seeking wisdom of God, who ever liveth to make intercession for them, and giveth wisdom to them that ask, and upbraideth not.

Neither do men reason wisely that it is right to do what minds are capable of doing in affinity with evil. This produces error, discord, confusion and death.

Man's capacity to act brings with it a just law of action. Men are bound by the most sacred bonds of law to act right, the same as God is, each in their sphere of action. The volition of mind, its capacity and power, with its inherent law, constitute the man a moral agent. To be less than what he is, he could not be a man created in God's image.

Being found in fashion as a man, Jesus became obedient unto death, even the death of the cross; for it became him to fulfill all righteousness. Christ is man's examplar. He was obedient to all law, physical and spiritual. He never sinned, for sin is the transgression of the law.

Obedience to law is man's duty. Power to do a wrong act does not justify action, nor the abuse of those channels open to men for their highest spiritual improvement.

The laws of nature are not explained in God's Word, but immoral acts are prohibited. If men would search the Scriptures in this light, they would soon see the reason why a certain course of action was proscribed in God's Word. That it was all the protection a finite mind could have against the penalties of the complicated laws of his being. None but an infinite being can fully understand all the operations and results of hidden laws. Hence the necessity of faith in God's Word, and obedience to his Word, to escape the penalty of violated law.

Thus God in mercy enjoined such duties upon man, as would bring to him the highest results of bliss and holiness if obeyed, and warned him in the most impressive manner of the effects of transgression.

Had man faith in God's Word, the knowledge of the law would not be necessary to secure his highest good. Heaven would reward the trust reposed in God's command. Then and only then, will man understand the necessity of the plan of salvation by faith. Mind, in its preparatory state, must take things upon trust, as one truth involves in its exposition many other things equally true and equally mysterious, which the finite mind can not grasp under its present limited advantages to explore infinite truths.

Man must be content to walk by faith in those things obscure, until the mind is developed through the sources opened to him, by the promised teacher of the Father, who will take of the things of God and show them unto him, as he is prepared to profit by them. The Lord with delight reveals himself in his works to his creatures, as they are capacitated to comprehend his ways. Nature and Revelation are not sealed books. Yet faith and trust are the only channels by which God can make this revelation to the soul.

The parent suits his promises and prohibitions to the capacities of his child; yet he knows the effort would be fruitless, for him to explain the philosophy of his own existence, of his own works: how he does exist, why he does exist, and why he requires obedience of his weak, ignorant child, and why disobedience is not equally his privilege with obedience, before he can secure the love and obedience of his own offspring.

The helplessness of the child moves the compassion of the father toward it, and prompts the command to save the ignorant one from sorrow. Then if the heart grows perverse, partakes of forbidden evil, and the child dies, disobedience inflicts its own penalties. The father grieves; he has no pleasure in the death of the child. He has done what he could to save the little being, who was, like himself, endowed with a will; but the child was perverse, because he chose to be, and died because he was perverse, not because his father did not love him, not because his father's counsel was not wise and good.

The foreknowledge of the father, knowing the nature of the law which was to constitute the child amenable if created, could not make him wish his race to be brutes, or machines, or any thing less than what they were, responsible, intelligent beings.

If one child disobeyed, another might be obedient and add to his glory and its own eternal felicity.

The possibility of disobedience, or the certainty of disobedience of some member of the family, which his foreknowledge might bring, would not justify him as their father to withhold from them an existence, or constitute them brutes, or machines, to act as they were acted upon, to prevent the possibility of disobedience of one or many.

The obedient were entitled to the full advantages of their high calling and destinies, irrespective of the use others would make of the gifts of God.

Thus, you see, to capacitate man to take the places of fallen angels, to hold companionship with God and angels, he must be subject to the same laws and penalties which all holy intelligences are, if he is also a candidate for their supreme felicities.

There never can be but one eternal, self-existent, all-wise God; for all the eternal perfections are by their affinities united to constitute this perfect Deity, who can not change.

The affectional nature, or love, as developed in the Son of God, is the offspring of the moral perfections of Jehovah; consequently like them, is in unison with them, yet possessing an independent free-will, like the Father, who presides over all the moral attributes constituting the Trinity. The Son, coexistent with the combined union of these moral attributes, which union produced the result named, *viz.*, the offspring of the moral perfections, which he denominates his Son, who is the express image of his person (his moral attributes being his person), which love nature affectionately and obediently obeys, the complicated laws of each and every moral attribute, which wrought in harmony with each other, constituting the self-existent, all-wise God, the everlasting Father, the Prince of Peace.

"No man knoweth the Father, but the Son, and he to whomsoever the Son will reveal him."

CHAPTER XVII.

SOUND IS THE CARRIER OF THE WORDS, THOUGHTS, AND FEELINGS.

Ques. I do not understand how words and thoughts can be revealed by sound, as previously described?

Ans. The spirit or motive in thoughts or words, has an affinity for the vitality of the air which is breathed, or nature could not support life. When thoughts are breathed, these affinities uniting produce at once their true image or picture, good or evil. First, the force of the respiration or breath breaks the air, when the affinities unite which give rise to the impulse expressed in words or thoughts.

By a law in nature, the affinity of thoughts conveyed by the breath, uniting with its like affinity in air, imprints at the same moment the character of the thoughts with the sound of the words, thus giving thoughts, words, and acts a character, good or evil, which are conveyed by sound, attracted by other elements in space possessing stronger affinities for such a record than the surrounding air, which receives the impression or impulse of thought. It is conveyed thither by the force of attraction and repulsion in sound, when air is put in motion by the breath, and stands thus daguerreotyped in space, a perfect likeness of just what the motives were which gave rise to the thoughts or words.

Nature is true to herself. Light, sound, air, are the channels of record, while space is the leaf of the book on which the true record of man's life is made.

The heavens are not pure in His sight, and shall be rolled together as a scroll.

Ques. Why are not the heavens pure in the sight of God?

Ans. There, in infinite space, stands the fearful record of man's life. That every secret thing under the sun shall meet the doer in judgment, whether it be good or evil.

Ques. How may I know this is so, since the Bible is silent as to the manner in which the record is kept?

Ans. The fact is given by God himself in his Word. Man's daily experience corroborates these statements, in the effects produced upon the mind of the saint and the sinner. The manner in which the record is kept is new to you, nevertheless true.

When words are spoken meeting with God's approval, the same law which imprints man's acts, gives also the character of the Divine approval, side by side. It must necessarily be so. The same law of natural and spiritual affinities in life, which unite to convey through that medium from earth, to its opposite pole in the heavens of space, the record of words, thoughts, and acts of each individual, will, before its mission ends, bring back to the mind, with lightning speed, the Divine approval or disapproval, if the mind is watchful for the impression.

These are most solemn and important truths, which should be kept before the mind, to arouse it from its dreamy stupor upon this subject.

God has condescended to advertise man of the fact of

such a record being kept, to induce him to be watchful and circumspect.

When men are brought before earthly tribunals, the most reckless are awed and influenced by the fact, his words are recorded, which will be a witness for or against him, procuring life or death.

Is it probable that God will give a man a breathing-place on earth, without providing a place for him in heaven?

And if positive affinities in spiritual life, as well as in the physical world, imply negatives, how reasonable to suppose there is, some where in yonder space, a place appointed by the Creator, which shall correspond to man's thoughts and acts, to receive the impress, or picture, true to life, of all the thoughts, words, and ways of man. Earth and heaven are opposite poles. Man can no more escape the record, than he can breathe without air, or see without light, or think without life.

The laws which make this record are as fixed and unchanging as Jehovah. Not one wrong deed committed is omitted; not one wrong suffered is forgotten. Even the kind act of giving a cup of cold water, is had in remembrance.

The injuries, injustices, and oppressions of avarice and lust, committed by man upon his fellow-man, makes up a fearful catalogue of crimes. How much man will need a Saviour to wash away his guilt and cover his transgression, before that fearful record is brought to bear upon his future destiny, when the Mediator shall sit as judge, and these books are opened, to judge every man according as his work shall be, whether it be good or evil!

Let the mind be watchful over its words, thoughts, and acts, also watch for the response of God to all he does and says; by this can the soul know when his ways please God. Hence the importance of the injunction, "Whether ye eat or drink, or whatsoever ye do, do all to the glory of God."

When the thoughts or words of man are put forth without a pure motive, the state is an unsafe one. Let the soul take heed, and seek to know and do the will of the Lord in all things. Why this indifference, fearing neither God's approbation or condemnation?

If men are willing to be taught, they will soon ascertain the truth of their position. When the soul sins, the shadows fall; they feel the Divine displeasure. Never rest, never close your eyes in sleep with the stains of conscious guilt upon the conscience. You had better never have been born, than to die with one sin unrepented of, unforsaken, or unwashed in the atoning blood of the Lamb.

In the judgment, there will be no more concealing of naked facts by professions of good, no garments of fig leaves wherewith to cover their nakedness. In view of this did the angel of the covenant say, "I counsel thee to buy of me gold tried in the fire, that ye may be rich: white raiment, that ye may be clothed, that your nakedness do not appear."

Ques. How can thoughts be impressed upon air, and come under the law of sound, to be recorded in yonder space?

Ans. The principle of life in nature acts upon the spirit of words sung, or spoken, or unspoken, as the rays of light, for example, act upon a transparent body, converging the rays to a focus, which gives the likeness to the object upon which these converged rays strike.

Ques. What is this principle of life in nature, which acts upon thoughts, &c., which is termed organic life?

Ans. The vitality of the air when breathed, is one principle. It is not necessary for the external ear to be conscious of sound, before nature's guards or sentinels can take cognizance of her loyal subjects, or mark her disloyal ones.

"The heavens and the earth will sooner pass away, than for one jot or tittle of the law to fail." "For every vain and idle word that man shall speak, he shall give an account thereof in the day of judgment."

Sound and motion is the camera in the air, which receives and exhibits the internal objects or character of thought from the breath, upon the same principle that the camera in the arts exhibits external objects by the power of light. The same power that conveys the diversity of distinct sounds of conversation to the ear, infusing the spirit with which it was spoken into the mind, also conveys it yonder, to be reserved in living characters like life, of the motive and thoughts, as well as words and acts. If there is an affinity in the listener, the mind feels a sympathetic response, if not, and it is repulsed, the mind feels the impression made by the opposing influence of words and spirit to itself. This is the effect of both natural and spiritual law acting in concert in union or repulsion. If the mind is passive, the impression is deeper than when resisted; if in sympathy with it, either good or evil, the influence is strong and mighty. Nothing can break evil affinities thus formed but the power of faith.

Nothing can disunite good affinities thus happily met but unbelief, suspicion, evil surmisings, or uncharitableness.

The penalties, or abused sources of good, lie heavy upon the transgressor. He is both corrupt and courrupting. The influence of a rash or idle word, from one reputed to be wise and just, is a stench in the atmosphere of wisdom and consistency.

Your friend, in his argument against this teaching, makes no distinction between the law upon which sound is based, and the sound produced, thereby denying thoughts, as well as words can be reached, making sound both the effect and cause. The spirit is made conscious from internal impulse, as the external ear is of external sounds.

Law in nature is adapted to mind as well as body, to thoughts as well as words; while words fitly spoken, breathed in the spirit of love and meekness, are jewels transfixed in other minds, imperishable as good, eternal as duration.

Ques. Can the law be abused by hearing, &c?

Ans. Yes. He that listens to evil communications with approval, without rebuking the same, is guilty with the communicator, if he suffers sin upon his brother unreproved.

The just man will always let his light shine (*i. e.*), his influence be felt, whenever sin can be put to shame. When the sinner is incorrigible, then the grace of silence is the light that must shine. These combined laws of nature and spirit are intimately connected with mind, and are the channel of communication between man and man, God and man (for faith comes by hearing), between man and Satan; for evil thoughts proceed out of the heart, and from the abundance of the heart the mouth speaketh.

But for sound, the organs of speech and hearing would be of no avail to the human family. The laws of sound are also the channel of intuitive instruction to the mind from spiritual influences. The suggestions of thought to the mind, are words spoken to the inner ear of the soul. The soul listens, is influenced, and feels as sensibly the effect of impressions, as if spoken to the external ear.

Internal vision is also a channel of communication, as well as external. The Divine approval and disapproval, is as clear and manifest to the senses of the soul, as the written or verbal words of friends are when read by the eye, or spoken to the external ear, then conveyed to the mind. The result is the same upon the mind, whether the communication be external or internal. The bodily senses constitute man a social being among men; they qualify him for happiness, improvement, and usefulness; they open up new and varied resources of enjoyment in the physical world.

Independent of these, the mind can be reached by spiritual influences through the senses of the soul, that correspond to those joys and sorrows that come to the soul from external objects, yet exceeding them in spiritual delights. The word of the Lord came unto the Prophets. The Lord spoke into Samuel's ear the things he wished him to know.

"Take no thought what ye shall speak, for the Holy Spirit shall tell you in that hour what ye shall say."

"That that is spoken in the ear, proclaim ye upon the housetop."

Scripture abundantly testifies this is the manner of the Spirit's teachings. Said the man of God, "I will hearken and hear what the Lord God will speak unto me." This was as often to the inner ear as the outward; for others standing by heard not the words.

It is in this way Satan suggests evil thoughts to the mind. Therefore Christ said, "Resist the Devil, and he will flee from you." "Draw nigh to God, and he will draw nigh to you."

If evil spirits are listened to and yielded to, the soul is wounded and slain by sin; sin revives, the soul dies to good. Paul said, "Truly he had not known sin, but by the law." The carnal mind being the channel through which he was assailed and overcome.

These avenues of the spiritual senses (*i. e.*), intuition and perception, were given to all minds for the perfection of their nature; both being channels for communion with God and spiritual intelligences in time and eternity. Angels possess the same powers of mind and capacity to communicate to mind both from impulse and perception. So do departed spirits, as Moses and Elias appeared in the mount, and talked with Christ in reference to his sufferings and death. Gabriel appeared to Daniel and talked with him; so did the angels at the sepulcher.

Words are both vocal and suggestive, according to circumstances. So God has spoken to the world by his Word and by his Spirit; both are based upon the law of mind and nature.

As well might the idolater multiply his idols, in disobedience to the law, because love is the basis of idolatry, as well as the basis of the atonement, and then meet in circles to worship, consulting the image as his oracle to enlighten the world on spiritual things, as for those who neglect to go to God in the present manifestation, and seek wisdom from sources where it is not to be found. "Let the dead bury their dead, follow thou me;" (*i. e*), when the dead are buried, leave them. You have done your last work for them, and they for you, unless employed by God with the angels to minister to you as the heirs of salvation.

Such, if called to you out of the divine order, will do you no more good than Samuel did Saul; while the law which you would violate by convoking the departed, would bring its curses upon you. The evil which an evil thought, or word, or act, attracts by its evil qualities, in affinity with the prince of evil, is stronger than the human will, even. There is only one power stronger than the power of evil affinity (*viz.*), that power is faith, that can dissolve every link in the chain, and let the captive go free. "The law of life in Christ Jesus hath made me free from the law of sin and death." "So he that walketh after the Spirit, shall not fulfill the lusts of the flesh; for to be carnally minded is death, but to be spiritually minded is life and peace." Here the law of affinity with sin, is the law of death, which can only be annulled by the omnipotent power of faith.

CHAPTER XVIII.

THE LAW OF SPIRITUAL MANIFESTATION AS ACTED UPON BY EVIL SPIRITS.

You now see that the law in spiritual manifestations by sound, is neither miraculous nor supernatural, in the sense in which these terms are generally employed, but based upon nature's laws, as old as creation, and also adapted to the law of mind, coexistent with Father, Son and Spirit. "For he spake and it was done, he commanded and it stood fast."

Yet man and Satan may transgress this law, by making it a channel of evil communication with evil instead of good, without the aid of further supernatural power than each possesses by nature, or the sanction of the Supreme Being. When visible results are produced by evil agencies unseen, it is from the conjoint influence of minds in the body in affinity with evil unseen. Mind in the body is as invisible to the visible perceptions of man, as are the invisible agencies about him. Yet no one questions the fact that he has a mind, because he can not see it.

The past and present knowledge of evil intelligences must be great though limited. Then add to this their forecasting sagacity, prejudging of the future from the past, and you find in every evil spirit a mighty foe to good. Is it surprising, then, when the spirit of self in man attracts these evil spirits to himself, that many things from the past and present, and in the future, even, should be correctly communicated by them to man, when the truth at the time will serve their purpose better than error? This device of Satan has long been practiced upon the credulity of man to beguile into sin, by coming as an angel of light and knowledge, to deceive man by his apparent omniscience and omnipresence, to receive his teaching as truth. The soul needs spiritual light to understand his devices. Spiritual agencies know by the power of intuitive perception, as well as man, the operation of minds in concert with them, and can take from the past knowledge of such many facts and communicate it again by sound as well as by impression. This stratagem of Satan has often been met and overthrown in the meeting of circles, by the power of good angels present, to cover facts which they in their previous guardian care were more identified with than the evil spirits; thus crippling and limiting their knowledge of the past as well as of the future, to their prejudging sagacity, which is as fallible, after all, as their nature.

Angels do this to stagger and arrest minds in affinity with Satan to pause and consider, before they are drawn into the whirlpool of error. To defeat the plots and machinations of Satan and his allies, is mostly the only way good angels can aid and deliver minds from their power, who repel them by the violation of law, in seeking evil rather than good.

To retaliate for this unsought protection to man, Satan meets angelic influence and the teachings of the Holy

Spirit at all points; and if there is sin or unbelief in the heart, he throws in tares with the wheat, and both often grow together, until the soul learns to resist evil and die to self, and take for his standard in all things the Word of Truth, to try the spirits withal.

In circles where sounds are produced, or objects moved, if a strong opposing mind is present, by the determined effort of the will, the charm or circle of affinity is broken. This power of resistance God gave mind for its safety, and it is equal to any emergency, if the power is put forth in might, and is the only protection that can be given to mind against surrounding evil agents, who have equal power to use or abuse nature's laws with themselves. The sounds produced in the circles, called rappings, are made by the breath of spirits, the will directing it against the wall, the floor, or any solid substance which conveys sound better than air, moves the air, and produces the muffled sound when it comes in contact with solid bodies. The vibration of the air conveys the sound to the auditory nerve of the ear; the sensation is heard, and felt sometimes upon the body, instead of the mind, which is the more usual mode of satanic influence, and is the only way evil spirits can affect men directly under the restraints of grace, unless they yield themselves to their power by the transgression of some law of nature's God.

Ques. What is the difference in the effect between sounds conveyed through the air, and through solid substances?

Ans. Sound passing through solid substances can be felt by the body; thunder, for instance, shakes the building, and the sensation is felt as well as heard; not so if the person is up in the air. If lightning strikes the earth or any solid substance, the effect is the same. This fact in the circles, so often realized by individuals, is the result of natural causes, which the man wise in his own conceit ridicules as duplicity, because he is himself so deluded in ignorance of cause and effect of the laws through which unseen agencies operate.

The consanguinity of evil spirits when convoked would be fearful, were it not for repelling influences of restraining grace by guardian angels present.

Sounds can be as easily produced in accordance with nature's laws when not obstructed by opposing influences, or by placing objects which are non-conductors of affinities in their way, as you can breathe, sing, or speak at will. Yet if another stops your breath, you can do neither, though your will is good to do so.

Objects are moved in accordance with nature's law. The affinity between material objects and life, is the channel of operation. This channel is electricity and caloric in its latent form in the material object, through which spiritual affinities previously unite, in forming a circle of magnetic influence around, by placing conjointly hand seen and unseen upon the same object. The trio is formed of human magnetism (latent electricity) in the object, and spiritual influence, or motive power of spirit, in the spirits unseen. These encompassing the object several times, until the chain of power is complete, the object is moved at the will of spiritual agencies, or at the suggestion of individuals.

This law of communication is not evil; it is only made so by evil minds, in convoking the departed. It is, like other laws, made for the good of the whole, but in its misuse perverted to the destruction of reason and truth.

Because evil is developed through the evil, in this manifestation; because of the nature of the developments, for man to deny its truth or its source, is to say, the ways of God are unequal.

As well might the source of the rains, and dews, and the sunshine of heaven be questioned, because they nourish the tares that grow with the wheat, the noxious weed that chokes the tender blade of grass; the snow, the hail, the frost, because the sufferings of the destitute are increased by them; the fire, because it destroys; the water, because it drowns. Instead of condemning the source as diabolical, because perverted by the ignorance and free-agency of mind, human reason would be better employed in escaping the evil, by seeking such protection as obedience to the law will give.

Ques. Now, may I be taught where Satan's seat is, and what is his work in the present manifestation, that I may avoid his devices?

Ans. He cuts off the bud of hope from the true vine, and engrafts it into the strange vine, Antichrist.

He reiterates the same doctrines he did to Eve, "Thou shalt not surely die. Ye shall be as gods, knowing good and evil."

The pen of false doctrine emits a meager light to make proselytes

by the hands of men who disobey the law of spiritual life.

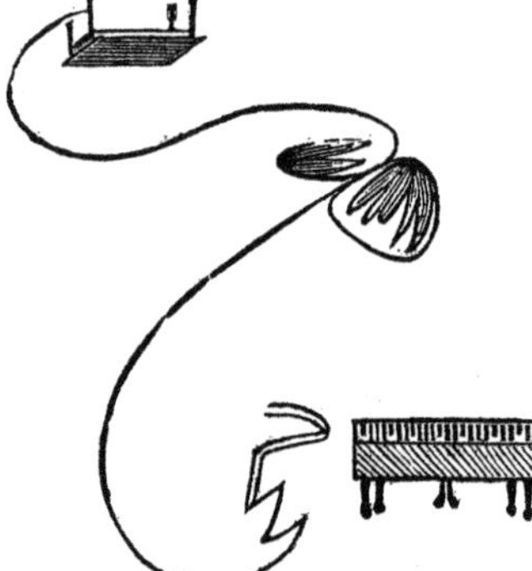

Their tables have become a snare, and a trap, and a stumbling-block.

The dragon and the beast, and the false prophets, know their time is short.

All these things are not of the Lord, but belong to Satan's devices to deceive man. Try the spirits. If an angel from heaven preach any other doctrine than that which is preached, let him be accursed.

Do you ask why was man subject to a law in nature, that gives evil such power over him?

Nature's laws may be compared to a highway, which was made equally free to all, and necessary for each to attain the same end, and the highest goal of happiness, both present and future.

No one can monopolize a highway open and free to all; neither can he turn out of the way, if he would see the end of his journey in peace.

In pursuing his way, he is liable to meet with travelers returning or halting by the way, who may use their influence to dissuade him from persevering in the good way. This liberty which other travelers take to intercept his progress, the same law gives him both the liberty and power to resist. Now do you ask why travelers are subject to such annoyances?

The free-agency of man explains this. The highway must be thrown open, or travelers so disposed could never reach the desired haven. The fact of the way being free to all, that all may be alike saved, does not compel all to go forward. Great inducements are held out to encourage the travelers to persevere. Yet they halt and turn back. This is the reason the traveler is subject to annoyances in the highway, but not to dangers, if he keeps his eye on the mark of the prize of his high calling, at the end of his journey. That will attract him onward with greater force than all the combined power of travelers who are returning; (*i. e.*) satanic power and travelers halting by the way. Earth and hell can not hinder or endanger the soul, if he will for himself obey God.

By this, you see, the power is yielded by man to Satan, or he could have no power over him. For he is a created spirit, and subject to the law of mind in nature, the same as man. The weakest intellect can repel him by resistance; yet they can not prevent his assaults. The law of mind is the highway.

Christ said of him, he goeth about like a roaring lion, seeking whom he may devour.

Now mark, here is an allusion by Christ of the way he devours: like a roaring lion; by the use of the laws of nature in sound, in accordance with spiritual life.

Satan suggests to the minds of the travelers in the highway to eternity, hard thoughts of God, the difficulties of the way; marks out easier ways. Thus men listen, halt, turn back. Satan in man, then, under his power, roars, pours out volleys of oaths, threatens, erects scaffolds, inquisitions, devours the souls of men whom he uses as his instruments to destroy the bodies of the souls he can not ruin.

Jesus knew the law of nature, when he put the natural life of man in the power of his fellow-man; therefore he said, "Fear not them that can kill the body, then there is no more that they can do; but rather fear Him that can destroy both soul and body in hell." Fear the effect of the power of sin, which destroys both soul and body in hell.

The penalty for sin has gone forth: "The soul that sins shall die."

In further illustration of this subject, Satan is called the prince of the power of the air, which worketh in the hearts of the children of disobedience.

"The power of the air." This includes the law of nature, which Satan misemploys as his agent in evil. The power of air is the only channel of direct communication between mind and mind, visible or invisible. Without it thoughts could not be expressed or embodied.

Satan has so long monopolized the thoughts and words of men, and sin has so cursed the physical world, as to cause the elements to war, under the control of the prince of evil. All this work of devastation is the result of evil, and Satan is the prince of the air over the evil.

The union of matter and spirit is based upon the laws of nature, by which God communicates his will to man, both through the external and internal perceptions; by which the Holy Spirit becomes the teacher of heaven and earth; by which angels communicate the will of God to man, which makes heaven and earth vocal with the songs of praise, and tunes the harps of the harpers before the throne.

This power filled Gabriel's trump at Sinai's Mount, and will again rend the air by the sound, "Awake ye dead, and come to judgment." It was the agent by which God's law was communicated to man.

Ques. How; was not the law written?

Ans. Sounds introduced the alphabet. It is the agent which keeps the record of the law, whether obeyed or transgressed. This will be the agent by which the assembled universe will each hear their doom, "Well done, good and faithful servant," or, "Depart ye cursed."

Still will it follow each class, and make heaven vocal with shouts of triumph, reverberated with sweetest songs of praise. "Victory, victory through the blood of the Lamb!" shall resound throughout heaven's wide domain; while hell will be vocal with the voices of despair in weeping, wailing, and gnashing of teeth, which is the second death.

The present manifestation is based upon nature's law, produced by the concert of action of spirits. Evil spirits can by the same power or law when convoked unite, as good spirits can.

The same power of the will that seeks good, when perverted, can convoke legions of evil spirits. Christ knew this law when he said, "If I should ask my Father, he would presently give me more than twelve legions of angels;" and *vice versa,* when the mind will, it can repel legions of devils, and draw nigh to God. You could have no power over me except it were given you of my Father. The power upon which the law of affinities in mind is based, and free-agency, is the secret of their power. Not that the Father turned against his Son, and gave these special license to conspire to reject and crucify his Son, whom his love and mercy had sent into the world.

When minds voluntarily convoke evil influences, and knowingly sin, then they stand upon the Devil's premises of abused law, taking their cause out of the hands of God.

To them, unless they turn from their transgressions, Satan is their prince. To them he has by their choice became their master, their leader, and does enter into league with them, to plot the ruin of the innocent and transgress every law of God.

The transgression of one command makes man a sinner and the servant of Satan. Therefore he said, "If ye offend in one point, ye are guilty of all;" or under the same penalty which the transgression of all law brings upon the soul — (*viz.*) death. "For ye can not serve two masters, for ye will either hate the one and love the other; ye can not serve God and mammon."

We have long wished to bring this solemn truth before the mind. The Christian churches of the nineteenth century are like the churches of Asia Minor; through lukewarmness and unbelief they have left their first love, to follow after fables, and it is high time to awake out of sleep and put away all sin by turning to righteousness. Christ the Lord spoke these words to that class or grade of sinners who were satisfied to make the outside clean by profession, while the inside was corrupt. Thus deceiving themselves, hiding under the plea as a covert for some cherished idol the incapacity to forsake all sin, and walk with God, who is the end of the law for righteousness to them that believe. Keep close to Christ by faith, and you will escape the devices, and snares, and power of the Devil.

But if the soul transgresses in one point, he opens the avenue of his heart to sin and Satan's power, otherwise he could have no power over man.

Since Christ was led into the wilderness by the Spirit to be tempted of the Devil, to save the world from his power Christ overcame him, and ever after, it is written, devils were subject to him. This power he gave his disciples and all that would believe on him, even unto the end of the world.

Fear not, ye tempted ones of earth,
Satan is a vanquished foe;
Your Captain leads his conquering hosts
On to perfect victory.
The lurking foes in ambush lie
Content; no more to meet your King
In open combat, on pinnacle or plain.
Their roaring power true faith defies,
And puts to flight alien powers,
And turns the edg'd sword,
And brings to life the dead.

CHAPTER XIX.

THE DOCTRINE OF THE FOREGOING CHAPTER ESTABLISHED BY SCRIPTURE.

WE will give a few Scripture proofs, how, by the agency of spirits, solid bodies are moved.

Disembodied spirits, angelic spirits, or satanic spirits, can move solid bodies; but it is in accordance with the unseen laws of nature.

Angels rolled away the stone at the sepulcher of Christ. The walls of Jericho fell without the instrumentality of human hands, but not without human aid. They encompassed the city seven times in faith before the walls fell. Here was the union of faith with God's promise — effect follows cause.

Jesus said to his disciples, "If ye had faith as a grain of mustard-seed, and ye should say unto this mountain, be ye removod into the midst of the sea, it should obey you." Here Christ asserts facts, not possibilities; yet reveals not the hidden laws controlling the fact, that man might walk by faith.

Again, "Where two or three are met in my name, whatsoever they ask, believing, it shall be done unto them." Here is belief acting in concert with the hidden cause producing the results.

He that hath said, "Walk by faith," and again, "Have

faith in God," knows well the results of such trust in his promise. Faith is to man what motive power is to spirits unseen. It is upon this principle that objects are moved. The affinities of mind between the unseen spirits and individuals convoking them, is sufficient, with the power of the will of the unseen agencies, to move objects. Else how could the faith of the believers, when in affinity, or in other words, in harmony with the Divine nature, remove mountains? There is no affinity without faith, nor faith without affinity.

Still further, the magicians possessed power to imitate the miracles of Moses by the same law; yet their faith was not omnipotent, for it possessed no affinities with the Divine nature, not being from above, but from beneath. The faith of Moses overpowered theirs, when put in competition with it. This is why Satan's works are lying wonders, not in obedience to the principles of truth.

It is upon this principle the power of one mind, of the opposite feelings with the circle in concert, can disturb their operations, if not prevent them.

This law of faith was given for the great good of mind. The positive of any affinity involves its negative; hence unbelief is the negative of faith.

To empower the will to believe imparts the power to disbelieve — the power to love, the power to hate. Christ could do no mighty works in Capernaum because of unbelief.

Faith is a creative power in nature, as well as in grace. By faith, we understand, the worlds were framed; yet the laws of the attributes of the Creator were the agent in the creation of all things.

By the creative power of faith was water turned to

wine. The same elementary properties were in the water, as supplied the grape with juice, with the exception of the additional qualities belonging to the grape above the water. This miracle consisted in adding to the element in nature other elements of nature in affinity with it, by the creative power of faith. This is called supernatural, or above nature. This evil spirit's can not do.

Thus the work of creation is in accordance with nature's laws, under the controlling power of an Intelligence superior to nature, and above nature. For this Intelligence can rebuke the winds and waves of the sea, and they obey.

The work of redemption was also on the same mysterious principle; the work of God by faith — "God manifest in the flesh." Thus redemption was based upon the law of nature and grace, privileging each individual arriving to the age of accountability, to be the arbiter of his own future happiness or misery.

In this life the happiness and wretchedness of individuals is in a great degree dependent upon their social and physical relations to men and things. Not so in eternity. Every fetter is broken when probation closes. Then the pure in heart enter into the full fruition of life. The present life is the preparatory state. As the state of the embryo is to the birth, so is the preparatory state to the future life. The present life as much depends upon the moral circumstances attending the embryo state for its happiness here, as the future state depends upon the moral state of this life for its eternity of happiness.

Thus, you see, the law upon which mind is based, to enable it to reach its highest capabilities in companionship with its God, is also open to the transgressor, if he choose death to life. Satan in alliance with wicked men of perverted minds, may perform many signs and wonders to destroy men. Their power is no supernatural gift; it is in accordance with nature's laws, subject to the Divine penalty.

This power of Satan over man since Christ's resurrection, is limited to the will of man. Satan can have no more power over man than is given him by man. Christ delivered the whole world from the oppressions of the Devil. Previous to Christ's death, the devils possessed the human bodies of men. They became lunatics, as men now do, by giving Satan power over them.

Christ coming in the form of a man, taking man's nature, who had sold himself to Satan, the Devil had power thereby, because he possessed the human nature of man, to take Christ up bodily and place him on the top of the pinnacle of the temple. This indignity Christ endured and met, all for man, that being tempted he might deliver them also which were tempted. Here he vanquished Satan. Ever after he went about doing good, healing the oppressed of the Devil.

Devils were subject to him; he died in the flesh to destroy the power of the Devil, then transmitted this power to them that believe, even unto the end of the world, by the laws of consanguinity; he being King of kings and possessing all power in heaven and earth, transmitted this power to man.

If Satan could take up Christ bodily, and angels can move solid bodies, as at the sepulcher, and the man of faith remove mountains, is it strange that spirits unseen, acting in concert with living men, should move solid bodies? While men remain moral subjects of law, this must be so. While probationary time continues, moral agency must; the one implies the other. When one ends the other must. When a man has run a race and won a prize, he is no longer a candidate for the prize; he has come in possession of it, and is the incumbent of the prize and its honors. He is no longer under the discipline or law of those running a race, but under another law, adapted to the change of his circumstances.

Thus, when we say his moral agency closes with his probationary race, we do not mean he has no volition, or has become like a machine, to act as acted upon; but that as a moral being, the opportunity for securing the prize was given and is past; and with the change of his circumstances, another law, suited to that change, meets him from the same necessity it has in the first and second stage of his being— (*i. e.*) before his birth until his death.

We wish to call your attention to this fact: no influence, good or evil, can produce such results as above named, with faith or without faith, in alliance with evil or good, without the agency of natural cause and effect.

Faith and works in the just man must go hand in hand. Faith uses nature's laws as her necessary implements, as the husbandman does the implements adapted to agriculture.

The life of faith is no visionary phantom, as many minds regard it. And to sweep away this error have the outward demonstrations been permitted, to convince of spiritual life beyond the grave, and the necessity of faith in Christ to overcome the evil in the world, and the power of sin and unbelief. But listen to the Spirit's teachings, directed to the mind of the sinner. The just man and the holy angels, owe all their power to God.

Even the Son, as Mediator, expressly declares, when his mission is fulfilled, "And all things are subject unto him that did put all things under him, and the last enemy is destroyed, which is death. Then shall the Son also be subject unto him, that did put all things under him, that God may be all in all."

Satan has no delegated power over the children of men, other than his once high vocation as a cherubim of glory gives him.

He was by nature empowered with gifts to qualify him to draw all classes of intelligences to the Father. These gifts are perverted by him in drawing all men unto himself, with the full consciousness of what is to be his doom. Since he encountered his defeat in heaven, and again on the pinnacle, he is a conquered foe — Satan can only work by proxy against God. Ever after he came supplicating and trembling before the Son, not to send him into the deep, saying, "Hast thou come to torment us before the time?"

He knows full well his time and the torment which is to follow, which makes him now tremble as he believes.

"Do ye believe that I am he," said Christ: the devils also believe and tremble. O! thou of little faith, wherefore didst thou doubt!

Thus, you see, the law of the present manifestations is based upon nature's law — as ancient as the attributes of the self-existent Deity; — transmitted to angels at their creation for their highest good, also to man.

The manifestation is only varied in the mode of its operations, making the good and evil of spiritual things more tangible, acting upon external objects through the media of the same influence as the mind has previously been acted upon.

It is an open door to the secret hidden springs of the law of mind. The law is one thing, and the results of obedience another, and the results of disobeyed law quite another

While you may say the law is from God, the results produced from transgression are not from God. Error and insanity are the result of man's work in league with Satan. Though "hand join in hand, they shall not go unpunished," and though city be joined to city, it shall not stand. And if men receive the developments made through minds destitute of saving faith in the Holy Ghost, in preference to God's word, they deceive themselves, and pierce themselves through with many sorrows.

By the same law of consanguinity, Christ had power to impart his love — nature to man, and give those that believe on him and abide in him, power to do the works he wrought. The same power in kind as he received of his Father, he gave to his children.

So also have evil spirits power to impart to their willing servants, the spirit of their evil natures, and are truly called by Christ the children of the Devil, "for his works they do."

The law of consanguinity adds to the weight of responsibilities. The parent justly claims obedience from the child. The child justly claims protection from the parent. "Thus it is written, if a man provide not for his own household, he is worse than an infidel." He violates the law of filiation and consanguinity who neglects to do this.

When a parent has made such provisions, and the

child breaks the laws of his relationship to his father, refusing his protection and service, saying, "I am corban, a gift," I am free from you, I am under no further obligation to serve or obey you—by this unlawful freedom he disinherits himself from his father's protection and possessions, and becomes the servant of another master.

It is written, "Moses' law said, honor thy father and thy mother; ye have made this law of no effect by your traditions."

The word of Christ, is, "Love the Lord thy God with all thy heart, and thy neighbor as thyself."

The spiritual laws of consanguinity and affiliation were shadowed forth by the law of Moses, to be such as exist between the vine and the branch, Christ and his people.

The covenant of day and night, seed time and harvest, shall pass away, before God will break his covenant with his people that serve him, or disinherit them, or leave them to the power of the Devil or sin.

At the same time, if men refuse Christ as their eternal life, they have no life in them; like the disobedient child, they break from all restraints of parental filiation, depriving the Father the privilege of feeding and clothing them, and themselves of the blessings of a Father's love and home.

"Because sentence against an evil work is not executed speedily, the hearts of the children of men are fully set in them to do evil." Had earth's probation closed at the fall, all that will reach heaven through the covenant of grace, would not have known its bliss. God could not be just in cutting off all those he had predestinated to life, without a probationary trial, no more than he could

Adam before he sinned; consequently he provided a Saviour, and protected man's free-agency by giving to each the offer and privilege of life. Then he proportioned future rewards to the trials and sufferings here, endured by reason of his social relations, which were unavoidable, while the free-agency of each was protected, to capaciate man for the choice of eternal life.

Any other arrangement but free-agency of the will, would have made the salvation of the servants dependent upon the master, the salvation of the child upon the parent, the subject upon his sovereign's will. The work of man's salvation was too important to each soul, created for such high destinies, to be left to the caprice of another's favor or will, while their temporal and social relations must necessarily be dependent upon each other.

Thus, you see, the great I Am, which is above nature's law, has rescued the sinner from the just penalty of sin, and still spares and perpetuates human existence, until all the souls he predestinated to have a being shall live, each in their day and generation. And they are to have with the first Adam an equal choice ultimately for life and happiness for what is suffered now by the curse entailed; they shall be more than recompensed by the reward that shall follow the faithful.

While the sinner who rejects salvation, "it is written, he counts himself unworthy of eternal life;" and perpetuity in an eternal existence of misery, if immortality were given, would not be a blessing, when there was nothing to hope for beyond his present evil state. So God in love as well as justice hath said, "The soul that sins shall die." This death is not annihilation of spirit or matter, but a dissolution by the power of the second death, of the conscious individual existence resolved back into first elmentary principles in nature, and life and breath, which first constituted the man a living soul! When spirit and matterwerebrought together by the creative power of God, the result was called life (*i. e.*), it became a living soul; when resolved back again to elementary principles, the dust returning to dust, and the spirit to its elementary existence, this is called dying to the soul as a conscious individual. God hath said, I create and I destroy. The soul that sins shall die. The suffering which this dissolution must cause the soul, is not the purifier nor the atonement for sin; it is not the suffering which purifies, but suffering is that which destroys eternally: an eternal death from which there is no resurrection to life.

Ages on ages roll their rounds, while the penalty is being executed: "In dying thou shalt die," suffering according to the deeds done in the body.

The hopeless despair in the consciousness of the loss of the glories of immortality and eternal life; the fearful looking for of judgment and fiery indignation, with the addition of the sufferings and injustice they have caused others to feel, when united with them in their social relations in probationary life, and the effects of such injustice in bringing others to the pit of death, these are their fearful reward, while "The wages of sin is death."

These considerations brought to bear upon the conscience by the reflex acts of the laws of nature, mind and memory, in affinity with past scenes, impressing all minds at the same moment, who have acted a part in corrupting and destroying the innocency, the happiness, and well-being of their fellow-men; in this way reaping what they have sown. Having sowed to the wind they reap the whirlwind. Having sowed to the flesh, they of the flesh reap corruption.

This is the only harvest the works of self in alliance with Satan can produce. A poor harvest indeed are the wages of sin and unbelief, which have cut off the bud of hope and engrafted it in the strange vine, Antichrist, to be gathered and burned, with weeping, and wailing, and gnashing of teeth. When the last scene is enacted, and the loss of life is bewailed, they each witness the destruction of their destroyer.

Those most vile endure an amount of anguish proportioned to their iniquity, their cup being filled to the extremity of their endurance from moment to moment. This suffering is not the inflictions of an avenging God, but the effect of sin. He hath said, "I have no pleasure in the death of the wicked;" and expostulating, said, "Turn ye, turn ye, why will ye die."

All is the fruit of their own doings. "The way of the transgressor is hard," for they shall "eat the fruit of their own doings;" fixed laws of mind and nature are their own executioners and destroyers. "The murderer hath not eternal life abiding in him." "He that hateth his brother, is a murderer." How terrible will be the torments of those who are reserved under chains of darkness, unto the judgment of the great day! As by the same law of mind the effect of their machinations against all flesh shall react upon them, each remembrance filling each successive moment their cup of misery, to their utmost powers of endurance, until the Devil is destroyed and his deluded subjects behold his end. "For the end of the wicked is destruction." In their death struggles, with weeping, and wailing, and gnashing of teeth, "they shall call for rocks and mountains to fall upon them and hide them from the presence of God and the Lamb."

The consuming fire of God's love shall cause the mountains to flee away as vapor. Then shall come to pass the saying, "The Devil and all his works shall be destroyed." "The wicked shall be ashes under the soles of the feet of the righteous, in the day of his visitation."

"The last enemy, which is death, is destroyed." Then ends the mission of the Lord Jesus Christ as both mediator and judge. And again, "He enters into the glory which he had with his Father before the world was." "The glory of the only begotten of the Father, full of grace and truth."*

NOTE.—Created life is an accommodating term, used in the writings, to express the creation of the physical and spiritual powers and capacities of man, in their adaptation to life. Life is uncreated because emanating from God—rather than being the work of God. The manifestation of life in the physical universe of matter, is in form, pulsation, and motion. This is called creation, so the manifestation of intelligence and spiritual life in the universe of mind, is called the creation of mind, or the living soul—yet the life which organizes and vitalizes and permeates matter, is distinct from matter; for when this life is withdrawn, matter loses its form and vitality and returns to dust—so the mind which animates the created capacities and powers of the human soul is but the manifestation of mind and intelligence from the great First Cause—and the soul is as dependent upon it for its continuance, as the physical organism is upon life for its individual preservation.

The manifestation of mind, is mental action—thus men are capaciated to think, reason and reflect—to will and obey. God wills man if obedient to live. Man's spiritual creation is the manifestation, or the effect of the mental action of the Spirit of God, giving volition and individuality to mind—creating capacities and powers, in the human soul, in the likeness or image of his adorable attributes, yet finite, because created and dependent upon the same cause for perpetuity of being as it was for its creation. God gave life conditionally.

"If He gather unto Himself His Spirit and His Breath, all flesh shall perish together, and man shall turn again unto dust. Thou sendest forth Thy Spirit, they are created, and Thou renewest the face of the earth."

Men make no distinction between the sustaining and vitalizing principle of life, imparted from God to man, and the created capacities and powers of the individual mind which is the soul, whereas the two are as distinct in their equality and individuality, as the machine and the propelling power of water or steam which puts the machinery in motion.

The soul is dependent upon this life for existence, yet the soul is not the life, nor the life the soul, any more than the dynamic power of water or steam is the machinery it propels, or the machinery is the water or steam because it is propelled by it.

This life cannot be corrupted by man or devils, for it is uncreated, undying and incorruptible in its nature—yet the soul and body may be corrupted and death follow, as the result of the withdrawal of life by the Giver.

This subject will be treated more fully in a future volume.—*Note to Page* 165, *line* 10.

* See Appendix, Note E.

CHAPTER XX.

THE LAW OF LIGHT AND KNOWLEDGE.

THE law of mind is the basis of truth to man's understanding. He opens the storehouse of wisdom by his willingness to be taught divine truth from the books of nature, Revelation, and Providence, which are adapted to his three-fold nature.

These are the trees of life on this side of the river, of which men are invited to eat and live for ever. But of the tree of knowledge of good and evil (*i. e.*), from sources where there is a mixture of good and evil, man may not eat, because he can not wisely separate the evil from the good, the truth from the error.

Let men leave these mixed fountains, such as are opened by clairvoyance and consultations with the dead, and not rest in them, but look through these to God, as the great source of life and light. Then, in affinity with holiness and faith, will every good gift of God become a pure stream of life to the soul. Nothing is to be refused, nor called common or unclean; no truth is to be rejected because it is perverted by others, in using it in a way and for purposes it was never designed to be used.

With rocks and stones man may fortify his towns and protect his defenseless head from storms; but he can not convert stones into bread, conveniently, and if he should, the benefit would not repay the trouble.

So man may learn many things from tables, from convoked spirits, based upon the law of nature; yet the knowledge is unsatisfying, being of mixed qualities. Still again, he may learn through the medium of a transfer of mind (*viz.*, clairvoyant) into spiritual circles, in affinities with his own mind.

When spiritual subjects, good or evil, absorb the mind, unseen influences associated with the subject of thought are attracted to the mind; if the will is yielded the nervous system is brought under the control of a superior force, and thus that system is brought under the influence of good or evil, from the knowledge of those minds from which they are receiving instruction, corresponding to the moral state of the heart, whether from the human mind, or spirits unseen. Also he who learns of God the truth by the same law, must be in spirit as a little child, teachable, passive like clay in the hands of the potter, willing to be moulded into vessels of honor or dishonor. Truth, not self, must be his one idea.

He can not be attracted by holy affinities as was Paul, and John, and Peter, up to the third heavens to learn unerring truths, unless he were like them baptized with the Holy Ghost. These were given as samples of holy communings of the apostles with the heavenly hosts, for the benefit of the church below.

These instances on record show the facts, not the possibilities of the spirit being caught up into heaven, before it was dismissed from its clay tenement on earth. "Whether in the body or out of the body," Paul said, "I can not tell." While Peter said, that he was "in a trance." And John, the revelator, said he was "in the spirit on the Lord's day." Ezekiel and Isaiah in vision saw the throne of God high and lifted up. Jacob in a vision, saw the angels of God ascend and descend. Stephen, as he looked up steadfastly into heaven, saw the glory of God, and Jesus standing on the right hand of God.

These are recorded facts of Revelation to be received by men. These were wrought through the agency of the Holy Spirit, the teacher of heaven, the promised gift of the Father to the children of men.

These facts show man was so constituted by nature, that by the laws of mind, he was capacitated to be influenced by holy inflences such as God saw fit to employ, in their proximation to the Deity; that by the use of the powers given through these instrumentalities, man might rise in the scale of intelligence, to hold companionship with angels and God, by being assimilated into their spirit, and thereby new aspirations kindled within, to seek more earnestly after the knowledge and likeness of the Son of God.

Without this law of mind, man could never have been saved. He failed in rendering obedience to the law of his being, which was a transcript of the Divine Mind. There was no other way left whereby man could be saved, but by the faith or power of assimilation. "Christ in you, the hope of glory." "Except ye have the spirit of Christ, ye are none of his."

"If any man keep my words, I will come into him: I will bring my Father with me, and we will sup with him and he with us." "Know ye not your bodies are the temples of the Holy Ghost, whose temples ye are?" "He that defileth the temple, him will God destroy."

"Present your bodies a living sacrifice unto God, holy acceptable, which is your reasonable service." "Except the spirit of Christ dwell in you, ye are reprobates."

The Jews knew this law of mind, for when they rejected Christ, they said, "We will not have this man to reign over us, for he hath a Devil, and casteth out devils by Beelzebub, the prince of devils."

Believing him a false prophet, they feared to imbibe his spirit. Christ met this by saying, "If I have done evil, bear witness of the evil; but if good, why persecutest thou me?" These Scriptures prove that Christ's spirit must dwell in his children. Thus, you see, the law of mind admits of another spirit or spirits possessing and controlling the human mind in its probationary state.

When Christ said to the devils, in the possessed, "Who art thou?" they replied, "We are legions." Also another fact illustrates this truth; "A man taking to himself seven spirits more wicked than himself, they enter into and dwell there; and the last state of that man is worse than the first."

Satan's seat is in the carnal mind. The carnal mind is the lusts of the flesh; it is not subject to God's law, neither indeed can be; therefore it must be slain. The appetites and passions of the animal man must not control his spiritual nature (*i. e.*), his affectional nature.

When minds are possessed with the spirit of the Devil, they do his works, the fruits of his spirit are manifested; anger, wrath, malice, strife, envyings, evil surmising, evil speaking, hatred, variance, murder, adultery, sorcercy, witchcraft, lying, deceiving, and if there be any other evil work, it belongs to his selfish spirit, which he communicates to man.

This evil heart of unbelief is not God's work. It is no part of his creation. He is eternally opposed to all sin; his open hand opposes it, his power repulses it at every turn. The price paid for man's redemption shows his hatred to sin and iniquity.

There are many facts in Scripture showing that Satan's seat is in the carnal nature of mankind, prompting him to make a God of his appetites, or some ruling passion of the animal man. Satan found an easy transit from the debased human nature of man into the swine.

If men would judge of themselves, they would know which master they served, Satan or Christ.

When the evil spirit is cast out, men will sit at the feet of Jesus, clothed and in their right minds, "Being cleansed from all unrighteousness, sprinkled with clean water; cleansed from all filthiness of the flesh and spirit; perfecting holiness in the fear of the Lord; having no fellowship with the unfruitful works of darkness."

When the law of affinity existing between spirit and spirit, and between spirit and matter, is better understood, an ocean of light will be poured upon the human intellect. What is now thought impossible and improbable, will prove to be simple and consistent with nature. It is the ignorance of law that darkens mind.

Body or mind disobeying the law of its nature must incur the penalty of law. Yet the sin of ignorance is winked at; that is, God does not impute the sin of willful transgression to those who ignorantly break the law. Many are sincere seekers for truth.

But why should minds resort to these mixed sources for knowledge, when the Lion of the tribe of Judah prevailed to open the sealed Book, and open before man, not doubtful sources of instruction and erring teachers, but he has opened the treasures of knowledge, and gave man the key of the storehouse of wisdom, that by keeping the commandments, they might find their reward, and avoid every doubtful source which leads to sin.

He also sent a teacher to be man's instructor into all truth, in every thing pertaining to man's best good. Why pervert the best gifts of God, by following the devices of Satan?

These various states of body and mind are developments of the law of mind and its affinities for kindred minds, and are reliable or false, according to the moral and spiritual state of the minds and their affinities. If clairvoyance could have been reliable, while the soul lives in sin, then God would have used it, instead of speaking himself to the patriarchs, and prophets, and apostles; and after, by promise, sending the unerring Spirit of Truth to guide men to living fountains of water, and give them to eat of the bread of eternal life.

These laws controlling human magnetism, thereby bringing the mind into a state of spiritual vision, would subserve the best interests of mankind, both in aiding the science of medicine and developing the science of mind, if properly employed and used for the purposes for which they were designed by the God of nature.

God never designed these sources as the oracle for the soul when originating between finite minds independent of the Holy Spirit, but for the developments of science pertaining to body and mind, that he might choose the good and refuse the evil, and receive such spiritual aid as man's physical and social relations require.

The gifts of God are perverted, and their tables

have become a snare, and a trap, and a stumbling-block.

The forcing of strength bringeth forth weakness, and the forsaking of truth brings error; putting out light brings darkness. Weakness, error, and darkness, bring sin, insanity, and death, to the willful transgressor.

"The law of the Lord is perfect, converting the soul. The testimony of the Lord is sure, making wise the simple. The statutes of the Lord are right, rejoicing the heart. The commandment of the Lord is pure, enlightening the eyes. The fear of the Lord is clean, enduring for ever. The judgments of the Lord are true, and righteous altogether. More to be desired are they than gold, yea, than much fine gold; sweeter also than honey, or the honey-comb. Moreover by them is thy servant warned, and in keeping of them there is great reward."

The painful results which follow the honest investigations of minds, in the present spiritual manifestations, is the penalty of violated law; error and insanity are nature's penalty. God pitieth the blindness and presumption of his creatures, in the course pursued. The law controlling the manifestation is abused, as the law of love is abused by the idolator.

The intellect alone can not by searching, find out God; spiritual things must be discerned by the spirit. God, then, is the source to which minds should go to be taught all spiritual truths; seeking first the knowledge which cometh down from the Father of lights. Then the acquisition of earthly knowledge will flow into the mind easily and naturally, from the legitimate sources, so amply provided by the God of love, who knoweth you have need of all these things, and in his good providence will add them unto you. "He that seeks, finds," when he seeks from the right source.

Thorns do not yield figs, or a bramble-bush grapes; neither can a corrupt fountain send forth sweet water. Then, how can man find out knowledge of witty invention by consulting the dead, when the Word of God expressly forbids the practice?

"God is not the God of the dead, but of the living;" (*i. e.*), God is not in the wicked dead to give knowledge to the living. For he ever liveth to give to them who ask, and they that seek shall find. "Thus it is written, seek ye the Lord while he may be found. Call ye upon him, while he is near. Before the evil days come, or death draws nigh, before the silver cord is loosed, or the golden bowl is broken at the fountain, or the pitcher at the cistern." Life is the time to seek the Lord. Death changes man's circumstances, but not his nature.

"He that is filthy, let him be filthy still; he that is holy, let him be holy still. As the tree falls, so it lies;" this is nature's law, none can change it, not even God. If he should act contrary to nature, he would cease to be God.

NOTE EXPLANATORY OF DRAWING FOURTH.

THE opposite drawing was given upon the inquiry of the writer, as to the final results of this manner of the Spirit's operations, when rightly understood and practiced by the believing heart. Those hints written from dictation, and truths taught by those who are led by the Spirit's teachings, will bring out of the treasury things new and old, which would call honest minds upon both continents to the subject of the soul's privilege, and as far as the law of spiritual life was believed and obeyed, would make each heart like unto a well of salvation, out of whose fount shall flow rivers of living water, led on by the Holy Spirit, increasing in love, faith, purity, and charity, until "their light should go forth as brightness, and their salvation as a lamp that burneth," as represented by figures given in the drawing.

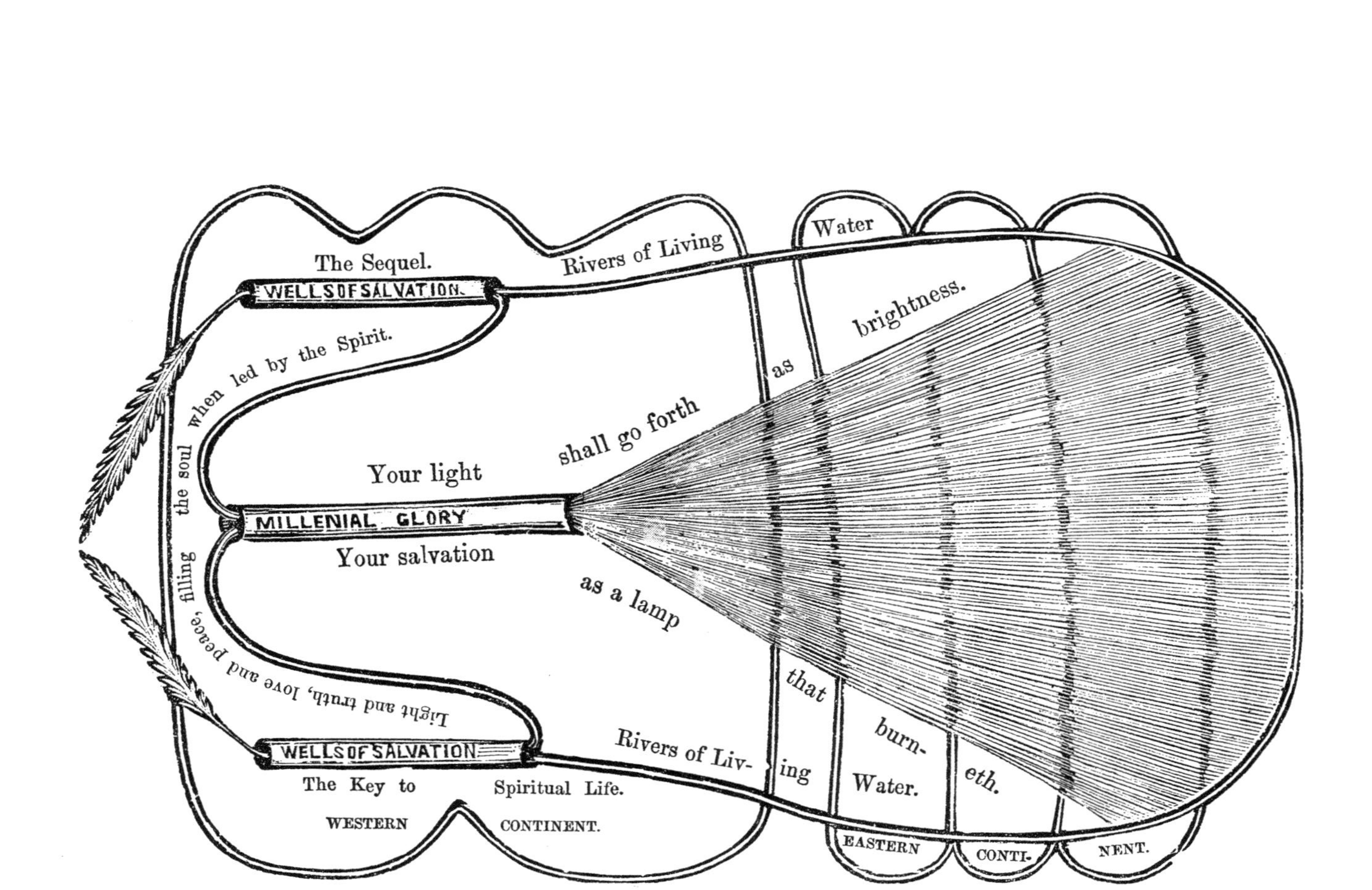
Light and truth, love and peace, filling the soul when led by the Spirit.
WELLS OF SALVATION
The Key to Spiritual Life.
WESTERN CONTINENT.
MILLENIAL GLORY
Your light shall go forth as brightness.
Your salvation as a lamp that burneth.
WELLS OF SALVATION
The Sequel.
Rivers of Living Water
Rivers of Living Water.
EASTERN CONTINENT.

CHAPTER XXI.

CONCLUDING ADDRESS TO THE READER.

It may not be wholly uninteresting to the reader, to know something more definite of the manner in which the writer was first led to investigate this subject, as well as the course since pursued, to arrive at such different conclusions from other writers.

Previous to the announcement to her, which was wholly unsought and unexpected, June 10, 1851, that she was chosen a medium, as it was termed, and could write under the dictation of spiritual agencies unseen, she was entirely ignorant of the existence of such pretensions, or the possibility of the fact. She regarded it as an impossibility, and a shocking assumption and deception, and so expressed herself to the individuals present, wondering at the apparent candor and credulity of those professing to be thus influenced. And to convince those who averred that she could be thus influenced, she took the pen and held it passively, desiring to use her influence to put down what she considered such a presumptuous act to deceive others.

The first sensation experienced, was like that produced by the galvanic battery — a benumbed prickling sensation; then seemingly the hand was moved through this influence upon the nervous system; letters were formed, sentences were written, purporting to come from the departed.

This greatly surprised and astonished her, doubting whether she did not do it herself, after all. She then took the pen a second time, when the same results followed. Repeating the experiment in the secrecy of her own family circle, and with a few friends, who were as incredulous as herself, she wrote many things, of which her own mind was as unconscious, until written, as were the lookers on.

This mysterious influence was variously tested, by the few in the secret with her, until their unbelief in the facts was compelled to give place to the force of evidence.

This point being settled, the next step was to ascertain the source of the influence. Here arose new difficulties, which called down many unexpected and painful trials. In the integrity of her heart, she stated facts to some few divines and professional gentlemen, inquiring whether it was the result of the operation of her own mind, upon some hidden law unknown to her, connected with Psychology, or was it what it purported to be, from spiritual agencies? It is not pleasant to dwell upon the reception her confidence and sincerity met with from such sources. Repulsed and ridiculed by those who were teachers in spiritual things, overwhelmed in perplexity, yet required by the conscientious convictions of her own mind to persevere, in her ignorance and helplessness she went to the Lord and to his Word. There she soon found the practice of consulting the dead was forbidden.

The gift of the Holy Spirit was the sent of God — the promised teacher of the Father to the world; to him she was taught by the writings to look, as never before by the teachings of man. Heretofore she had done as others did, calling upon those whose names were given to communications written, and writing upon whatever topic the importunity, curiosity, and suggestions of other minds, as well as her own, presented. This course, to her, was pregnant with error and evil. At this period she took a decided stand, not to ask curious questions from that source, or recognize any such oracle as valid, but to look to God alone.

From this time the nature of the writings changed, her course was approved, her doubts and fears began to vanish. She earnestly sought by prayer the law controlling the manifestations, and was assured it should be given her, if she no more called upon the departed, or yielded to the importunity of individuals, as she had done, to gratify curiosity, or give tests of its truth or source. This course displeased the Lord, and caused him to withdraw his protection from her.

As well might the man of God be required by the unbeliever to give a test of the power and truth of his alleged belief in the efficacy of the prayer of faith, and then base upon the facts by him then furnished, the truths or falsity of his theory, as to require tests to prove the truth of spiritual affinities of good and evil. Both must inevitably fall back upon the truths and facts developed already, which were based upon God's Word.

She was directed particularly to persevere, and as her own mind was prepared to comprehend and digest the instruction given, new light upon the law controlling these now mysterious developments should in due time be given, and then she would know why, and how, error and truth were mingled, why evil predominated, likewise know the design of God in requiring her to follow, or be led by this influence, in this untrodden path. According to directions, from this time, June, 1852, she kept a Journal, and wrote when drawn to do so, as circumstances would permit.

To her this heavenly teacher has thus far been a safe guide, enabling her to part with all human helps and props, and so overcome what opposed this manner of the Spirit's operations in her heart, that the trials endured to learn these divine lessons, are doubly repaid by present blessings and helps received, as she follows on to know the Lord, day by day. In more than one sense, can she say (according to the promise given), months before her days of mourning are ended, "The sun does not decline, nor the moon withdraw its light;" sorrow and tears have given place to joy and gladness. "The truth makes free."

The writer expects to meet in judgment all herein written, and in her might of faith says to shrinking nature, from thus giving her testimony to the public, upon so unpopular a subject as basing the truth of spiritual manifestations upon the laws of nature and a holy life, be still! Though an atom of earth, a dust of the balance, yet as such an atom, and as such a dust, to God alone belongs the homage, and the fear, and the worship of her undivided heart.

She has given her little all to God, as a free-will offering, for this cause of truth, "Every where spoken against." She has sacrificed to God her time, her labors, her reputation, her friends, and ventured out upon this new track, because commanded in the Word thus to venture and to learn of Jesus and the Holy Spirit in all things pertaining to this life and the world to come, that she may walk the narrowest "narrow way." She is dilligently using these as means of grace, and as helps in the way of discipline and preparation, adding to patience godliness, brotherly kindness, and charity; that these fruits may be in her, and abound to the glory of God.

To such as will say of this manner of the Spirit's teachings, it is the height of assumption, delusion, and fanaticism, let us in return say, we no where limit the teachings of the Spirit to the manner of its developments to us; but try the efficacy of thus venturing out, upon the promises of the Word, for wisdom and light, yourselves. Venture fully, freely; "let no other trust intrude," and with us you will praise God; and like Abraham, you will be willing to go out alone, "not knowing whither you go."

Hoping the Spirit of Life, which has quickened her own soul, and made every yoke easy and burden light, may so dwell in the words written as to produce the same happy results in the heart of every one that reads, which these teachings have produced in her own soul, that those who, like her, have cherished the sincere desire to walk in the narrow way that leads to life may, by the hints given, be quickened in their onward course.

She earnestly hopes her halting and slowness of heart, to venture out upon the promises of God to guide those that put their trust in him into all truth, as is manifest in the extracts given, will prove a warning to others, if they would have the work of preparation cut short in righteousness. "For it is written, blessed are they that believe, and yet have not seen."

Would to God that every sorrowing heart could know

the safety and consolation this way of the cross brings to the soul, when its barriers are once overleaped, that they may steadfastly rest upon the rock which lies beneath the billowy waves and storms of self, as they successively roll over the crucified soul, without moving it from its moorings, or changing its purpose from seeing the end of its race.

She hopes no individual who may read these pages will impute to her the assumption she no where claims, of being infallibly led or inspired, as were the apostles.

The Word, we regard as most sacred, and the basis of all truth. The power to write prophetically and infallibly was imparted to but a few. That the individuals who wrote the Law and the Gospels were infallibly inspired for that very purpose, to communicate a standard of truth to the world, is cordially believed.

Upon the law of mind as given, one readily perceives how the mind could be so fully absorbed and taken up with divine truth, as to write as moved upon by the Holy Ghost, without any mixture of error from opposing influences. This she regards as the infallible state of the holy prophets and apostles, being sanctified and set apart by God for that special purpose, not contrary to their natures, but in accordance with it, to be a mouth and witness for God to the people.

Her position is very different; she is still a learner, and not a teacher in Israel; while this manner of the Spirit's teaching or speaking to the soul, is a universal gift of the Father to the believing church and world, and is the birthright of every believer who will follow the voice of the good Shepherd in the soul.

When, like hundreds of others, she was made conscious of this unknown power to write, at first, by yielding the hand passive, afterwards, when the mind had become disciplined by this patient waiting attitude, the manifestation took another form (*viz.*), like one listening to another, without any exercise or effort of mind, other than an interest to understand what was spoken, writing rapidly, hour after hour, not critically, but practically, she again earnestly sought for the law of mind controlling this new developed power. The explanations, as given to her, are submitted to the reader in the preceding pages. The intuitive powers are the channel of the Spirit's operation; and she fully believes that the "Lord still reigns, that the earth might rejoice," as the Scriptures declare; and that the Lord has not given the world and man up to the delusions of Satan (as many suppose), because minds are earnestly and sincerely investigating these manifestations, which were brought under their own observation.

She has persevered in her urgent plea for truth, until satisfied that the vein of truth has been struck, and as such she gives it to the world to explore. This mine of truth is deep and rich; its treasures are yet untold.

This manner of receiving instruction from the Lord (*viz.*, of listening to learn), may not please all, therefore such will feel called upon to reject it. Others may approve of the method, yet disbelieve the possibility of all minds being taught as here advocated. To both these classes of minds, we say, the future will prove to other minds, if not to yours, the truth of the law given, and future ages will concede the truths and facts herein stated, after the writer and objector have both passed away from scenes where obscure truths, which now shroud the mind in doubt, will become self-evident, fixed, and eternal, and as such be received by man.

It can not be denied, that the docrtines herein taught, are based upon God's Word, and sustained by numerous passages quoted in their easy and natural relations, without forced constructions, simply taking the Word as it reads; although differing from all known creeds, yet embracing parts of each. This fact has obtained her consent to publish the above extracts from her Journal. What is truth belongs to God. If there is error mixed with truth, that belongs to her mixed, fallible state.

The high position taken in the writing has been weighed by her with solemn awe; yet repeated assurances have been given that all that is here claimed, is the privilege of every believing heart, that she is by no means a special favorite of Heaven because thus led. All minds are capable of being taught by the Spirit. "The called," when fitted and made willing, "are chosen," because made ready to do the works of God.

The writer knows full well how to sympathize with those who have pursued a different course from herself—who have been perplexed in their honest investigations of facts, as presented to them in the so-called spiritual manifestations of the day, which shroud the subject in so much mystery, and which, in many cases, bring upon its advocates so melancholy physical results and profitless experiments — profitless both to science and religion — that its most ardent and fearless advocates have felt disappointment at the uncertain and slow developments made to obtain knowledge through these sources.

Could she gain an audience with individuals who write under this influence, she would earnestly entreat them not to call upon the departed, nor angels, but to look to God alone; then the results would be more satisfactory. When their mind is in union and harmony with divine purity, then they can claim the promise of the Father, "That the Holy Spirit shall lead the soul (thus waiting upon him) into all truth, and shew them things to come." Perhaps little by little, as in her own case; yet the patient waiting is at last met with satisfactory compensation, in truths given. Then, if the Lord send the departed, or angels, it is well. Let the Lord send by whom he will, all is to be received with thanksgiving, as Jesus received the angels in the hour of his agony, and as he had previously met the departed Moses and Elias, on the mount of transfiguration. Yet he did not convoke these in the hour of his crucifixion, but said, "If I should ask my Father, he would send me more than twelve legions of angels, to deliver me out of your hands." He always prayed to the Father for all things; and he has said to us, "Be careful for nothing; but in every thing by prayer and supplication, with thanksgiving, let your request be made known to God." "Who giveth to all men liberally and upbraideth not, and it shall be given him."

These holy ones violate no law of God, when they minister to man. If we would enjoy their protection, we must be in harmony with God and obey his law, otherwise we repel good and attract evil. God has given to man the ministry of angels; yet they are not to be his oracle, nor his God, but his helpers.

God is jealous of his glory; he hath said, "I will not give it to another." Let us honor him, and not lean to our own understandings, or be influenced by new circumstances or developments to strike out a path for ourselves, contradictory to God's Word. Let us yield and obey this holy Word, as the truth and the way. Thousands have ventured out to sea upon this foundation, and gone happily and safely home; while all others have made shipwreck of usefulness and happiness who have discarded its enlightening beams, its chart and its compass.

They have either been swamped in the oblivion of infidelity, or wrecked upon the barren rock of unbelief, or the quicksands of Antichrist, and materialism, and chance. Her sympathies are deeply awakened for those who receive the teachings they get through these mixed sources, in preference to the plain letter of the Word, because the agency is spiritual.

Error may by spiritual agencies be engrafted into the soul; but still error bears its own fruit, as in the engrafted tree in nature. "By their fruits ye shall know them," said the pen of inspiration. There are many such wild branches bearing their own fruit, even after they have been engrafted into the good olive tree. The reason is, the root does not bear the branch, nor does it impart to the branch all its life. The branch repels the nutriment the root contains, and only takes such as will not exterminate the errors in the belief and practice it most loves. Such believers are but partly saved.

Such engrafted branches as will not part with their evil affinities, for the good which the root contains, will at length become withered branches, and must be cut off, and gathered to be burned. The fruit which such engrafted branches bear, is immature and sickly; it never benefits him that gathers it, nor him that eats of it. True, it stands in close proximity to truth, and is an engrafted branch into the root of truth, and is shaded, perchance, among the luxuriant branches of truth, thus mixing and mingling the wheat and the tares together, until the harvest, when the reapers will gather first the tares to be burned, and then the wheat, or the fruit of truth, into the garner of the Lord.

Where is the church corporate, or the individual heart, even, that does not as tenaciously cling to custom as to truth, when they can not find, a "Thus saith the Lord" for its inference, even, because they love the tradition of the fathers, being educated to revere it; regarding it as essential to distinguish the peculiar sect or creed of which they are a member, or a branch?

These are the works that must be burned up. And happy will it be for souls when the sifting time comes, if there is any wheat found which will be saved, even as by fire, when their works pass this ordeal.

This solemn truth, so plainly taught in God's Word, and enforced in these teachings of the Holy Spirit, arrests the solemn attention of the writer, and carries her above the fear of man and out of the sectarian views of her own party church, and fixes the decision unwaveringly in her own mind, as to fearlessly break from such traditionary belief as conflicts with the Word of God; that she may not heap up (instead of treasures) the rubbish of hay, wood, and stubble, to be burned up at the last day, not substituting the teachings and commandments of men, for the commandments of God, not resting in works without the true faith, nor in faith without the accompanying obedience and submission the Gospel requires.

In this these teachings make no exceptions for churches or individuals, but regard all as in a mixed and unsafe state who practice good and evil, holding truth and error. The truth is blessed for its own sake, while the error breeds discord, strife, contentions. Yet the whole is cherished and sent forth by man into the world as zeal for the truth, when it is only error incorporated into the same body with truth, and clothed with garments stolen from truth; so that man embracing truth, new or old, requires much moral courage to extricate himself from error, and stand out naked and alone, aloof from popular theories, knowing how deaf the ears of the populace are to the heart-searching calls of truth, to put away all sin, and awake to righteousness, that they may be in readiness when He cometh, who "baptizeth with the Holy Ghost, and with fire, whose fan is his hand, who will thoroughly purge his floor, and gather his wheat into the garner; but who will burn up the chaff with unquenchable fire."

That the votaries of truth may lose nothing by the fire and the flames, the cry of truth in the manifestation has been made to the whole world. The world is divided into self-seeking parties, who jeopard their eternal interest and close their minds to the truth that makes free, for popular eclat, and traditions of men. These also sacrifice their own chosen friends before the shrine of their power, if they depart from their party interests and views to advance the truth more purely, than had previously been engrafted, by the fathers, into the creeds of their church. Such branches bring forth perishable fruit, each after its own kind, like the tree of self, from which it was taken. These do not profit by the assimilating power of truth to change whatever is not opposed to being changed, into its own likeness, that the branch may bring forth fruit like the root, which will bear the winnowing fan and purifying flame of Him that cometh after, and tries man's work, of whatever sort it is.

In concluding these remarks to the reader, the writer hazards an opinion of the future benefit to be derived by the world, from the present seemingly unpropitious developments of the age, which are the subject of the preceding pages.

The fact that corrupt fountains have sent forth, and ever will send forth, bitter water, until the fountains are purified, or dried up, does not disprove that by the same law, under whose control these waters flow, other sources may send forth pure and fertilizing streams, making barren and thirsty lands standing pools of living water. The developments of evil, as well as good, will make more tangible the truth advocated, and show each individual that he is a subject of the spiritual law of life, and that he can not depart at all from the pure fountain of truth, without cutting himself off just so far from its fertilizing streams. That the secret and cherished love of the human soul, whether good or evil, are the media or channels to him, of surrounding spiritual influences, whether satanic, angelic, or divine. Capacitated as man is, by the gifts of grace, to obey the spiritual law of his being, and love the Lord his God with all his heart, his neglect to resist evil and seek good, brings him under the power and dominion of evil, while he pursues the evil he loves.

When minds are made fully conscious of the fact, that by indulging in evil and uncharitable thoughts toward God or man, they instantly attract to themselves evil which is opposed to God, from the spirit world, which binds the soul so strong in the chain of sin and unbelief, "that when it would do good, evil is present" to prevent, then will they more intelligibly and steadfastly resist evil, and seek good by a determined effort of the will, and by the sword of the Spirit and the shield of faith, which are the unconditional gifts of God to man, which he must use to enable him to meet the conditions of Gospel salvation, and repel his spiritual foes, and thereby attract divine influences, which will break every fetter, and deliver the soul from Satan's power, and make of the captive sinner a new-born child, a free man in Christ Jesus, an heir of God, and a joint heir with Christ.

If the revival of the doctrine of justification by faith, in the days of Luther and Melancthon, and the doctrine of sanctification by faith, benefited the church in the days of Fenelon and Lacome, of Wesley, and Fletcher, we see not why a light that reveals more clearly the hidden springs, or law of mind, by which man is held a captive by Satan, a slave to self and sin, may not aid in his emancipation from sin and deliverence from evil, and become to man the medium or channel through which these great operatives of the Holy Spirit, *viz.*, justification and sanctification by faith, may work, to successfully cleanse the heart from all sin, and usher in the millennial glory; when human teachings will give place to the great teacher sent from God to man: "When one will not need to say to another, know ye the Lord, for all shall know him, from the least to the greatest." The child will as fully understand as the man of years, his danger from evil thoughts, and his remedy and safety in holiness, when this Scripture is fulfilled. "I am the Lord thy God, which teacheth thee to profit, and leadest thee by the way thou shouldst go."

Then from parental influence and example, holiness will become the watchword inscribed upon the posts of the doors, and upon the bells and bridles of their horses. "Then shall their m rchandise, and their hire, be holiness unto the Lord."

Judging from the writer's frail hold upon life, she may anticipate the call of her spiritual Joshua to pass over Jordan, before these pages meet the eye of many, if any.

To her friends, whose abodes she may no more frequent, she comes in these pages as formerly, a companion and friend, a learner at the feet of Jesus.

To the friendless poor and sick, whose abodes she loved to visit in life and health, but where her willing feet can roam no more, expressly for their benefit, and to supply in part her lack of service, which many years of ill health has prevented, she makes a free-will offering (more or less) of the avails of these published pages, to the use and benefit of the sick and friendless, any where, to be distributed in private charity, by the chosen almoners of God's bounty to her, who will most conscientiously appropriate every farthing as directed.

This volume, with the pages elsewhere alluded to. was penned in the hours of deep affliction and triumphant joy, in her invalid state, without human sanction or encouragement, in this manner of the Spirit's teachings, but, as she honestly believes, with the Divine approval.

These pages have been submitted to the perusal of a few Christian friends of different denominations, who have professed to be benefited spiritually by the perusal, and expressed a desire to see them published, that they might possess the work entire, and that others, also, might be benefited by the practical thoughts given.

The writer complies with the request, thereby hoping to secure a twofold benefit to the world; first, by giving temporal relief to the destitute, and secondly, by furnishing spiritual consolation to all who will receive it from this source.

She is encouraged to hope that these pages, when known, will make friends; and this encouragement arises from the reception they have already met with from the deeply spiritual. And she hopes that they will so increase and multiply in numbers, that like the five loaves and two small fishes of the lad, when blessed and broken by the benign Saviour, and distributed by his chosen disciples to the fainting multitude, before their race ends, they may feed as many thousands as did the loaves.

To her Christian friends in general, who have felt it dangerous to give her their countenance and sympathy in this work of the Spirit's operations, yet have borne her on their hearts to the throne of grace, she returns her grateful acknowledgments. Eternity alone can tell how much she owes to these praying friends, under God, for being saved in the hour of peril from making shipwreck of the faith, by refusing to be led by the Spirit in so new and untrodden a path; though the letter of their petitions has failed to be answered, in her desisting from the work, yet the spirit of the petition has prevailed, and she has been safely led on in ways she knew not, into greener pastures, and beside stiller waters.

To the few tried and faithful friends who strengthened and held her on her way, as alluded to in Chapter II., she owes much. When these pages meet their eyes, they will readily recognize their own portrait. May they be encouraged still to persevere, however dark to their future pathway may be the walk of faith. When they recollect the fulfilment of the promises made to them, let them thank God and take courage. While the great patience of the teacher, as exhibited in these pages, calls for a renewed and entire surrender of all, and for unbounded gratitude and thanksgiving to God, from the hesitating pupil, for all the unsought helps bestowed in times of need.

Being permitted to tender these expressions of her love and gratitude to her friends, and to the great Giver for every good and perfect gift bestowed, she now calmly and peacefully resigns all, and awaits her summons from this beautiful earth, and from the home of her loved ones, when her Lord and Master shall say, it is enough, come home. Or she is content to be detained still longer on the rough sea of time, and be driven out again to baffle with its winds and waves, even when seemingly just making port.

She fears not now to risk her little bark upon the sea of life, or even to meet the resistless waves of death, with such a pilot as Jesus, upon whose bosom she is permitted to pillow her lowly head, which shall bear her safely on to the desired haven of light and glory, where she hopes to join the church triumphant; "To come indeed unto Mount Zion, to the city of the living God, to the holy Jerusalem, to the church of the first born, to an innumerable company of angels, and to the spirits of the just made perfect."

Perchance while mingling her song of praise with this holy company above, who do the will of God in heaven, God may commission her with the exalted privilege to watch and water the good seed, which the reading of these pages may sow in some humble heart, until it shall bring forth fruit to the glory of God.

Perchance, too, as her surviving friends, one after another, "Shall lay down the cross to take the crown," she may be permitted to join the angelic band to welcome these tried and faithful ones to immortality's clime, and fall into the filed ranks of angelic hosts, as each is led up to the throne, "To behold Him by whose death they live."

APPENDIX.

NOTE A.

At this point the writer was apprised that the mind had become so disciplined by the passive waiting for the influence to move the hand, that henceforth she might write down such sentences as were given to the mind, in the same passive state she had written with the influence upon the hand the past year and a half; except when required to state facts that could be better illustrated by sketched delineations and representations, than by words, then the influence should control the hand.

That outward demonstrations were comparatively of little value, for these, like the sheet which was let down from heaven, "knit at the four corners, full of beasts," to instruct Peter in the will of the Lord concerning him, would like that pass away, and when compared to the effect designed to be produced upon the mind, were of small moment. The object was secured when the effect was accomplished; also outward physical demonstrations, were only illustrative of more hidden facts, in the spiritual work to be inwrought in the soul. (See Note B.)

NOTE B.

Some two months after the instruction given in note A, while engaged in sweetest contemplation upon the fullness of the atonement to expiate all sin, the following line, which was familiar, passed through the mind, so to speak, *viz.*,

"O! love divine, all love excelling."

To this sentence the mind was held without her being able to recal the next line, or verse, for an hour or two. When a convenient opportunity presented, she took her Journal to minute down passing events. As the above sentence was most in her thoughts, and expressive of the subject of her contemplations, she wrote it down; when immediately another sentence followed, not in rhyme, or what belonged to the verse, but had a connection with the subject. After a pause of a few moments, the other sentence was written; soon as finished, another, and another, was given, until several pages were written, none rhyming to her taste, yet the sentiment was full of meaning. Not knowing what to make of this either newly developed power, or a natural power newly discovered, she continued to write such sentences as were given. The measure of these sentences was sometimes given in rhythmical form, sometimes in prose, sometimes in blank verse. In no instance, however, was the verse finished in its diction, nor always harmonious to the ear. Yet the sentiment was pure, common sense, spiritual, and scriptural. Any attempt to improve what did not suit her taste, suddenly interrupted this flow of thought, and when left to her own intellectual effort, she soon found she possessed no more talent for correcting sentences given, if they did not please her taste, than for originating them in the first place.

This reconciled her to pen the thoughts that were given, since she was permitted to glean after the reapers, in "Boaz' field." The wheat among the tares, "Truth," was the pearl she sought. In this manner she wrote some three or four hundred pages, in her invalid state, not found in this volume, upon various subjects, both theoretical and practical, before the following pages were given, as explanatory of the law controlling the spiritual manifestations of the day, found in this volume.

NOTE C.

The Law of the Transmission of Good and Evil, as alluded to in Chapter VI., *page* 51.

Ques. Will this subject of the transmission of good from the parent to the child be more clearly explained?

Ans. Why should the doctrine of the transmission of good, more than evil, be questioned by man? Why admit the last and not the first, since Satan is the source of evil and God is the source of good?

Satan destroys, but God creates. Satan and evil are finite, while God and good are infinite. "He that is for man, is more than they that are against him."

"And did he not make one?" "Yet hath he the residue of the spirit." "And wherefore one, but that he might seek a godly seed; wherefore take heed to your spirit, let none deal treacherously with the wife of his youth."

"I, the Lord thy God, am a jealous God, visiting the iniquity of the fathers upon the children, unto the third and fourth generation of them that hate me, and showing mercy unto thousands of them that love me and keep my commandments."

The Lord appeared to Abram, and said, "I am the Almighty God, walk before me and be thou perfect. As for me, behold my covenant is with thee, and thou shalt be a father of many nations, and I will establish my covenant between me and thee, and thy seed after thee in their generations, for an everlasting covenant, to be a God unto thee and thy seed after thee."

"And I will give thee and to thy seed after thee, the land wherein thou art a stranger, for an everlasting possession, and I will be their God."

"And God said unto Abraham, thou shalt keep my covenant, thou and thy seed after thee in their generations." Then the covenant of circumcision was made as a sign and seal to Abraham's faith; signifying by the outward act the inward work, the circumcision of the heart by God, through virtue of the atonement made through his Son, to check and uproot the effects of evil upon the physical and spiritual natures of the rising generations, that they might be a chosen generation, a peculiar people, zealous of good works, and thus transmit derived good and the effects of good to their offspring, through faith and obedience, as Adam transmitted evil and the effects of evil, to his offspring.

This doctrine is taught in God's Word from beginning to end. It is co-eval with the doctrine of faith and sacrifices given to Adam, with the covenant made with Abraham, Isaac, and Jacob. It is taught in the New Testament by the apostles. The promise is unto you and to your children, to this end, that the descendants of Abraham, who were the children of promise, that they might be a holy nation and people unto the Lord.

God forbade the sons of his chosen people to marry the daughters of other nations, neither should their daughters marry the sons of the heathen and idolatrous nations, lest they turn away their hearts from serving the living God, and serve other Gods, thereby by their evil lives entail their evil corrupting natures of unbelief upon their offspring, as well as perpetuate the deranging and disorganizing effects of evil upon the physical world by unholy examples, and bring curses instead of blessings upon each. Is good less potent in its hereditary effects than evil? Is evil, that sprang from Satan, almighty? and good, that is derived from God, only mighty, casual, incidental, and transitory, when claimed and retained by obedient faith, as by Abraham, who believed God and it was imputed to him for righteousness?

To show the mercy and power of God to keep his covenant unto the children of faith, the Apostle in the Christian church introduces the subject by teaching the promise reaches even unto them and their children. When converts were made to Christianity, by one of the parties believing, it was said, the other should be sanctified by the faith of the believer, so as to secure the blessing of the covenant to their children, the Lord showing mercy and sending blessings upon thousands of them that love him. Yet when these depart from the faith, he hath said, "I will send a curse upon you and curse your blessing."

"Behold, I will corrupt your seed and spread dung

upon your faces, even the dung of your solemn feasts, and one shall take you away."

Here let us inquire in what way men suppose God will curse their blessing and corrupt their seed, but by withholding the promised covenant blessing, and thereby let their evil ways overtake them, to teach them he has no pleasure in their unrighteousness, or in their death, that they may turn and live.

Can it be believed for a moment, by the Christian teacher in Zion, this promise ends with the external rites of church organization, and leaves parent and child still unholy in heart and life to raise up a people, not only from whose lineage the Messiah was to come, but a people to serve and obey him?

Is this all God, by the gift of his Son, has done for the world, in destroying the moral effects of evil in the offspring of the man of God, who, like Abraham, obeys the law of love, and commands his household after him? God has done less good, after all, by the costly sacrifice made of his Son, than Satan has done evil, if man must necessarily live in sin, and transmit evil and not good to his posterity. This makes Satan more mighty than God in his chosen work, which is exalting evil and denying the power of God that bought them, despising his gifts of righteousness. Still, we say, how few claim the promise, and transmit covenant blessings unto their children, they rest in the letter of the Word, and satisfy themselves with the form of godliness, denying the power thereof. From such turn away.

Abraham, the father of the faithful under the law, began in the spirit; and shall the believer, under the Gospel dispensation, do less?

But there were false prophets also among the people, even as there shall be false teachers among you, who privily shall bring in damnable heresies, even denying the Lord that bought them, and bring upon themselves swift destruction. And many shall follow their pernicious ways, by reason of whom the way of truth shall be evil spoken of. "For if after they have escaped the pollutions of the world, through the knowledge of the Lord and Saviour, Jesus Christ, they are again entangled therein and overcome, the latter end is worse than the beginning." "For it had been better for them not to have known the way of righteousness, than after they have known it to turn from the holy commandments delivered unto them."

What is this holy commandment given unto Abraham and confirmed unto Israel for an everlasting covenant, and his posterity?

The true Israel under the Gospel includes all believers of all nations; and the great mercy of God is shown, by saying, "The unbelieving husband is sanctified by the believing wife, and the wife by the husband, else were your children unclean, but now are they holy." Confirming his word unto believing Israel, for an everlasting covenant. If facts prove that man is born in sin, it proves also that he has failed to keep his covenant vow with God, not that God has failed to fulfill his promises to him. If man, by his transgression of law, aided by Satan, corrupts his offspring as well as his friend, why not by obedience to the law, purify and bring blessings, rich and full, upon each, as well as curses? But it is happened unto them according to the true proverb.

"The dog is turned to his vomit again, and the sow

that was washed, to her wallowing in the mire." (Let him that reads make the application to the sexes.) God has promised them liberty and salvation from all sin, and the effects of sin. He has promised to save, to the uttermost, all that come to Him, and "that all things are possible to him that believeth." These are among the "all things;" yet they are the servants of corruption, and corrupt their offspring; for of whom a man is overcome, of the same is he brought into bondage. This is the source of native depravity, communicated by the transmission of evil, both by precept and example; not because it must necessarily be so, nor because there is no remedy provided and given to man, nor because man is not capable of meeting the requirements of the covenant stipulations; but simply because he believes not God's promises to him and to his offspring, and obeys not the law of love. Effect follows cause. "Man is conceived in sin, and brought forth in iniquity."

The holy seed of Abraham, who were the chosen people of God, to make unto himself a holy nation, are corrupted by unbelief, as were Adam's posterity by disobedience.

If men understood the Scriptures, they would preach Jesus as sufficient to destroy the man of sin in the soul of the believer, and urge him on to perfect holiness in the fear of the Lord; and thereby in the use of the power given them, created as they were in the image of God, with power to reproduce their kind, in the observance of the law to multiply and replenish the earth, he would by faith claim and receive the promise; for "children are the heritage of the Lord, and the fruit of the womb is his reward."

Said Paul to Timothy, "When I call to remembrance the unfeigned faith that is in thee, which dwelt first in thy grandmother Lois, and thy mother Eunice; and I am persuaded that in thee also. Wherefore I put thee in remembrance, that thou stir up the gift of God, which is in thee by the putting on of my hands."

Here is a recorded instance of the transmission of the grace of faith, from parent to child, from two successive generations; while Abraham was called the father of the faithful, and Christ the author and finisher of faith.

This teaching differs from the teachings of man, but it agrees with the Word. "For the righteousness of faith is not of the law, but under grace, and is able to make the comers thereunto perfect."

Evil communications are corrupting, in whatever way or form they are made, and one sinner destroys much good. These thoughts, with others before given you, of the effects of the great redemption wrought out by Christ, are but the outlines of salvation. Other great and weighty truths lie all along these boundaries, which speak of love and mercy to man.

The argument in these thoughts, is not that man can, by the righteousness of faith, redeem his own soul, or pay a ransom for his brother, but that he can transmit good, if he has goodness, by the same law he can evil, if he is evil. He can bring blessings or curses upon his posterity, according to his faith and practice.

This doctrine magnifies the power of God and the efficacy of faith, and strips from his character the unjust imputation of creating man a sinner, and then destroying him for acting out the impulses of his nature.

It vindicates his love-nature, and links together justice and mercy, which encircle his throne, while man is left without excuse for living in sin and perpetuating his shame.

Had the seed of Abraham imitated his worthy example, and retained the blessings derived through him, they would never have been a nation stripped, peeled, scathed, and dispersed, as in ages past. For God said of them. "For thou art an holy people unto the Lord thy God: the Lord thy God hath chosen thee to be a special people unto himself, above all people that are upon the face of the earth.

"The Lord did not set his love upon you, nor choose you, because ye were more in number than any people; for ye were the fewest of all people:

"But because the Lord loved you, and because he would keep the oath he had sworn unto your fathers, hath the Lord brought you out with a mighty hand, and redeemed you out of the house of bondmen, from the hand of Pharaoh king of Egypt.

"Know, therefore, that the Lord thy God, he is God, the faithful God, which keepeth covenant and mercy with them that love him and keep his commandments, to a thousand generations;

"And repayeth them that hate him to their face, to destroy them: he will not be slack to him that hateth him, he will repay him to his face.

"Thou shalt therefore keep the commandments, and the statutes, and the judgments, which I command thee this day, to do them.

"Wherefore it shall come to pass, if ye hearken to these judgments, and keep, and do them, that the Lord thy God shall keep unto thee the covenant and the mercy which he sware unto thy fathers:

"And he will love thee, and bless thee, and multiply thee: he will also bless the fruit of thy womb, and the fruit of thy land, thy corn, and thy wine, and thine oil, the increase of thy kine, and the flocks of thy sheep, in the land which he sware unto thy fathers to give thee.

"Thou shalt be blessed above all people: there shall not be male or female barren among you, or among your cattle.

"And the Lord will take away from thee all sickness, and will put none of the evil diseases of Egypt, which thou knowest, upon thee; but will lay them upon all them that hate thee.

"And thou shalt consume all the people which the Lord thy God shall deliver thee; thine eye shall have no pity upon them: neither shalt thou serve their gods; for that will be a snare unto thee."

But for this fact of the transmission of evil dispositions from the parent to the child, the redemption of Christ would take effect in the embryo; else all would not be made alive in Christ, as they have died in Adam, without choice or volition. Man begets in his own likeness, mentally, as well as physically. The evil dispositions communicated to the child, check the development of this free gift of life to man.

When the child is born, if these evil tendencies are strengthened and perpetuated by the example of the parents and those about the child, it goes astray from the womb, speaking lies, seeking out many inventions to gratify its inborn propensities, and becomes the child of wrath, even as others.

The same love and mercy which made provision for the redemption of man's posterity in the embryo, still follows him from his birth to the grave, with the enlightening and reproving influences of the Spirit of Truth, which enlighteneth every man that cometh into the world. If the child dies before it comes to years of understanding, he is saved; for Christ saves from the effects of the sins of others, where there is no willful transgression, because these effects were brought upon him without his volition, but from the necessary social relations of man.

Man begetting in his own image and likeness, is the original law of creation, carried out in all its bearings. Effect follows cause. The same law operates in the lower animal and vegetable kingdom, and in fact to some extent, in every atom of matter that unites to produce a new compound.

All matter, as well as spirit, imparts its affinities to the new compound or organization, which individualizes it as a specia or genera of the parent stock, or original compound. Each bearing fruit after its kind, thus classifying families in each kingdom. When the child comes to years of accountability, and resists the enlightening and reproving influences of the Holy Spirit, then another law meets him — the law of love, which holds him responsible to his Creator, and recompenses him according to deeds done in the body.

Even before the child is capacitated to judge of the nature of good or evil, and be influenced by motives of good to please God, it is met in its infant childhood and taught by the Spirit of Truth, whenever it does wrong, or follows the evil bent given to its nature by the transmission of evil from the parent. This truth must be conceded by every adult, whether Christian, barbarian, or savage, and shows the continued goodness and mercy of God to fallen man, to meet by his Spirit in the infant mind, the evil tendencies of sinful habits entailed upon him from his ancestors.

This provision protects the child even from the necessity of following the natural impulses of his evil nature, if its own little will yields to these good impulses and promptings of the great teacher. It is the work and office of the Spirit to erase and eradicate these evil biases in man's nature; and it will do so, if the will yields to its operations, independent of human teaching.

Here again effect follows cause. The child is instructed through his outward senses, his faculties developing slowly. Consequently he imbibes good or evil from example, as he has before by transmission.

If he prefer evil to good, these biases first received are strengthened, and become the roots of bitterness, and the gall of iniquity. If evil is resisted, his nature is changed by the action of the purifying fire of love, which element (*viz.*), love changes the action of affinities in spirit, as well as the element of fire in nature changes the action of affinities in matter.

The soul may be brought by the teachings of the Spirit alone, to a consciousness of its evil state by nature, and feel the wrath of God is resting upon him, not for what others have made him, but for what he has made himself, by yielding to these biases, against the light and importunity of the Spirit. He may so repent and believe as to receive forgiveness for past transgressions, without other teaching from man. This repentance for actual sins, does not eradicate the inbred nature of man's evil biases, or change his natural disposition; it only effects a change in his affectional nature, to love the good and hate the evil. This prepares the way for the Spirit's great work in the carnal nature of man. If the soul stops here, and is taught his work is done if he looses his first love from the temptations of the world, the flesh, and Satan, he soon returns to the weak and beggarly elements of the world, and is the same in nature as before; if not worse, he appears worse by contrast. If naturally covetous, he is covetous still; if dishonest, is dishonest still. The innate tendencies of his nature control him, when not controlled by grace. For a man will follow his love, let it be good or evil. He becomes a withered branch, seeking the gratification of his loves and lusts, quenching and grieving the Spirit by a determined opposition of cherished evil to the reasonable requirments of God's voice to him in his Word, works, and Spirit.

We have made this allusion to show what is necessary to eradicate the evil inherited from Satan by man, from man's free choice, and communicated from man to his offspring, by refusing to part with all sin.

It is the Holy Spirit that sanctifies and uproots evil, when self-love yields to its influence. It strikes at the root of evil, when its blows are not warded off by free-agency.

In the convert, the work is but commenced, when by repentance the self-will yields its opposition. If the work of redemption progresses in the soul, the Spirit brings the refining flame of love to act upon the roots and bitterness of sin, destroying the cause or root of evil thoughts and desires, as it has the effects of evil previously, by pardon and forgiveness.

When the soul is cleansed from all sin, it can no longer say, "when I would do good evil is present with me." The action of the baptismal flame which purifies, changes the affinities of the renewed spirit, like its refiner, by the same law of transmission. Therefore this complete regeneration, imparting the new nature when fully developed in a holy life, is called being born of God. He that is born of God overcometh the world; this is the test of this baptism of the Spirit. He possesses the new life and the unfeigned faith of a Timothy.

He that committeth sin, is of the devil. If purified, unless he abides in Christ, sin still reigns in the heart and affections, and brings the soul into captivity to the law of sin and death. Such a backsliding soul is not born of God. Though he was once begotten or justified by the Spirit, yet his new-life nature is not brought to the birth, or born of God, until perfected in Christ's image. But when the man of sin is slain, and the soul is risen with Christ in newness of life, as it is their privilege, sin has no more dominion over them. They are dead to the law of sin and death, which once stirred in their members.

"Whosoever is born of God doth not commit sin, for his seed remaineth in him, and he can not sin, because he is born of God."

"Seed," here, has an allusion to nature, the new life being in the seed, which gives the embryo its affinities and impulses corresponding to the nature of its life. This is as true of spirit as of matter; both are adapted to

27

moral agency. While the seed of grace, or the affinities of the Spirit remain in the soul, he can not sin, because his new nature is opposed to sin. Effect follows cause.

Man being a created being, body and spirit, he derives his nature from another. This nature possessed affinities like its Creator, until moral agency parted with its holy life, and then man became a transgressor and a dying soul; the affinities of his dying nature loved evil more than good. So again when moral agency consents to part with evil, he derives with the new life imparted, the natural impulses and affinities of the Author of this life, in proportion to the perfection of Christ's image in him.

There is no condition so fixed in probationary life, where if man cease to do well and falls from his steadfastness, but what the results or effects of his declension will follow. And his abiding in Christ is dependent upon his moral agency, and not upon God's sovereignty, now as at first, because the law of spiritual life is adapted to moral agency. It is written, "Keep thy heart with all diligence, for out of the heart are the issues of life." Trace human depravity to its source, as an evil perpetuated by man, not from necessity, but from choice. While all heaven is engaged in opposing evil, and rescuing him from its dominion and effects, which is death, let man co-operate.

"That which is born of the Spirit is spirit; that which is born of the flesh is flesh." "Except a man be born again he can not see the kingdom of God." If the unbelief and sin transmitted to the child checks the development of life, which the atonement of Christ brings into the nature of the child, as stony ground, and thorns, and briers, check the growth of wheat, and he lives past the age of infancy and childhood to accountability, having by actual transgression transgressed the law of love, as did Adam, though redeemed in infancy from the curse of the law, he must be born again of the Spirit, by yielding his heart of rebellion, or he can not be saved by justifying faith. Therefore the words of Christ are true: "Ye must be born again." That is as much as to say, to be saved from the effects of sin once, is not enough; if ye sin, ye must be born again, and abide in Christ, or ye have no life in you.

Provisions of grace are made to meet every emergency in man's probationary life, suited not only to his necessary social relations, not only to his lost state as a sinner, not only as a free moral agent, but all necessary provisions are made to meet the hindrances to a holy life, that it may no more be said, "The parents have eaten sour grapes, and the children's teeth are set on edge."

The child born in sin is not obliged to follow his evil biases of transmitted evil, as he would be, if there had been no Saviour or Holy Spirit provided. The Holy Spirit enlightens every man that comes into the world. This light is sufficient, if no obstructing influences were brought to bear upon the soul, to lead the child on in innocency in the pursuit of divine knowledge in time and eternity.

Since man hinders this work of grace in various ways by sin, so he is called by God when justified to advance the work of grace in the hearts of his fellow-men, to build up what man has destroyed, that he may lay up treasures in heaven. For he that gathers with him, scatters not abroad. It greatly enhances the happiness of man in eternity, to be a faithful steward of the Lord on earth, winning souls, rather than a corrupter of his race.

A state of innocency is not a state of condemnation, neither is it practical holiness, but a passive moral state, which is compared to good ground, a good soil for the sowing of the seeds of grace in the soul, which the Son of Man sowed in the field, which is the world. Such is the moral state of the infant born of holy parentage. Then if he add to this the practical holiness of obedience and faith, like Enoch and Elijah, he suffers not the penalty of natural death, but is not, for God translates him, when he is to be transplanted from this world into a more congenial clime of spiritual delights, where sin and sorrow can not come. These examples shine as a beacon light to earth through all time, to encourage the practice of virtue and truth in the fallen sons of Adam, to secure the same virtue, by holy lives of faith and practice. Observing all the law and the commandments, that they may secure covenant blessings unto themselves and their children, such shall shine "as the stars, for ever and ever." This figure means much. The redeemed child has by nature passive innocence instead of being created by God, or born wholly depraved, as men teach. The nature is innocent because redeemed by God; the transmitted carnal nature, which is ever at war with this good nature, is inherited from the flesh and spirit of the sinning man, begetting in his own likeness.

All good is from God. Evil, if in the soul, is there implanted by man, while the law of sin reigns in his members, which is the carnal mind in his flesh, he inherits from his progenitors which wars against the law of his mind, and brings him into captivity to the law of sin and death; while the inward man, that is Christ, who redeemed him from the curse of the law, is crucified by the carnal mind, aided by moral agency, and by him cast out of his heart, as he was cast out of the camp, and condemned and crucified by his chosen people.

Still, he says, all sin against the Son shall be forgiven. "Behold, I stand at the door and knock; if any man will open the door, I will come in and sup with him, and he with me." He stands as a Saviour to the whole world, and to all classes of sinners in the world, even unto the end; but proclaims the sin against the Holy Ghost shall not be forgiven. For he is man's teacher and sanctifier, not his Saviour. There is no forgiveness for refused light proffered by the Spirit of Truth, "neither in this world nor in the world to come." What man looses in time by the rejection of truth, is an eternal loss to him, even if saved. Eternity can not repair the loss. Therefore take heed, "quench not the Spirit." How strangely men speculate about the sin of the Holy Ghost, when Christ has said there is no redemption for that sin. How few but will suffer loss in this respect, yet saved as by fire. O, thoughtless man! grieve not the Spirit. There is a remedy for the sin of rejecting Christ, even until the eleventh hour, if he accept of life before probation closes. When pardoned, he is brought into a passive innocent state, justified; because justice is satisfied when the conditions are met. Then if he dies he enters the kingdom of heaven like the infant, to develop the nature given, and by the exercise of faith and love, there to add holiness or obedience to innocency; yet he shines not as a star for ever and ever, as do those who in early life seek the kingdom of heaven and its righteousness, and win souls to Christ. While treating upon the deranging and disorganizing effects of evil, we will repeat again the fact to illustrate the truth here advocated. The moral condition of the infant soul, as it comes from the hands of its Maker, redeemed from the curse of the law, Christ being made a curse for it, stands in the sight of law and justice in a passive moral state of innocency. *That is all Love could do for man*, until volition comes in, and by choice he becomes holy by practical obedience and aid of the Spirit, given to profit the soul, to lead it into all truth.

We said the moral state of the child was by nature a passive one, capable of receiving impressions from circumstances and surrounding external objects, without volition or opposition to good or evil, because it as yet possessed no power of volition to act, until its capabilities were developed. Its moral state was also innocent, because redeemed from the curse of the law, which the first transgressor had violated. The child was free from guilt, having never violated any law by transgression, for sin is a transgression of law; consequently the child could not be counted a sinner before God, but he is reckoned as innocent, until by willful transgression, like his first parents, he sins. Then he is a moral agent, having come to years of accountability. If he then loves and practices evil, he is no longer in the original state of passive innocency, but is a transgressor. Of such Jesus taught, except a man, not an infant or child, but a man, be born again, he can not see or enter the kingdom of heaven; and at the same time teaches, except ye become as little children, ye can not be saved.

Again, without peace and holiness, no man can see

the Lord. Holiness implies practical godliness of the heart. This is necessary to save the sinner, whose motive to every act is governed by his selfishness, which controls his will, and stupefies and deranges his reason and understanding, which was innocently passive at first, and a good soil for good impressions, if not corrupted by willful transgression.

Thus Jesus taught, "except ye become as little children, ye can not see the kingdom of heaven." Innocent in nature, passive in spirit, teachable, willing to receive derived good from the only source of good, that he may practice and perfect holiness in the fear of the Lord, and be as clay in the hands of the potter.

The kingdom of heaven, which may be said to be an active principle of righteousness, as well as a state of positive good, is put in harmony with the passive state of the child, and in contrast with the positive selfish state of the sinning man.

The kingdom of heaven is introduced into the parables of the Lord and Saviour of men, in this light: as an *operative principle*, imparting no evil but good to passive innocence. There, in that kingdom of righteousness, no evil influences can corrupt its passive teachable nature, and well might it be said, of such is the kingdom of heaven; for all that are born into that kingdom, when justified and sanctified, disclaim their own righteousness, and in passive innocency wait to be taught of God in faith, nothing doubting, when their waiting faith is imputed unto them for righteousness. The parable of the Sower teaches this doctrine:

"He that soweth the good seed is the Son of Man. The enemy that soweth the tares is the Devil. When any one heareth the word of the kingdom and understandeth it not, then cometh the wicked one and catcheth away that which was sown in his heart."

This represents one class of careless way-side truth hearers, never practicing what they hear, thereby cherishing evil instead of good. The stony ground hearers are another class, resting in an orthodox belief without reducing the same to practice; while he that receiveth the good seed among thorns, represents still another class substituting works of benevolence for obedience, for the righteousness of a present faith; but he that receiveth seed into good ground, is he that heareth the Word, and understandeth it, and brings forth, some an hundred-fold, some sixty, some thirty. Such are led by the Spirit of Truth, step by step, and overcometh the world by practical holiness.

At the conclusion of the parable you were taught the field or ground, in which the good seed was sown, is the world, while the different conditions of the ground alluded to in the beginning of the parable, represents the hearts of individuals in the world.

Here we ask, what makes this difference between good and stony ground, or between good and evil dispositions in the same individual, but the transmission of evil, since Satan or man can not create, but impart their own natures by sowing tares and catching away the good seed sown by the Son of Man, by the deranging and disorganizing effects of moral evil; thus transmitting evil, first, into passive, then willing minds, which is compared to stony ground, or to ground yielding thorns and briers?

This truth is also illustrated by the parable of the mustard seed, being the least of all seeds sown in the field, because passive innocence is the first state, or the smallest of all the seeds of the field in holy life, leading to practical holiness, which, in the adult, is called justifying grace. But when this seed is developed and grown, it is the greatest among the herbs, and becometh a tree, so that the birds of the air come and lodge in the branches thereof. We might convert this literal figure to spiritual truth, by saying, the angels or seraphims of light, which are represented as ministering to man, having wings, come like the birds of the air and lodge in the branches of the trees of righteous life, to guard the holy soul.

If God so loved the world as to give his Son to save the world, and Jesus said, "Lo I come to do thy will," *i. e.*, to save the world, then sowed the good seed spontaneously upon all ground, and beside all waters, after having paid a ransom for the ground, that is, the soul, and bore away the curse, that it might be productive and yield an abundant harvest; then if from the effects of moral agency, as at the first, it brings forth again thorns and briars, which is nigh unto cursing, whose end is to be burned, whose is the fault? There is no other sacrifice to be made for sin than that which is made, and if this is neglected, man as well as angel must meet the penalty.

What is the source and cause then of the biases of the human soul to evil, but the transmission of evil (last as first) from man to man? Has the Holy God entered into copartnership with man and Satan to originate and perpetuate evil? Does the redemption of the world mean only salvation by faith to the adult, and not to the child incapacitated to believe? No; while merciful provisions were made to reach those who should, from the circumstances above named, first be led to chose evil, then be willing from the convictions of truth to part with their evil for good, the helpless condition of a lost world was not overlooked. Yet except a man (not a babe) be born again, and become as a little child, passively innocent, redeemed from the curse of the law, that he may be made a partaker of holiness, he can not be saved. Sin being in the world affects man's social relations, as well as the physical universe in which he lives, and brings temporary suffering, and sorrow, and death, to all classes and conditions of mankind; nevertheless, the redemption of Christ in behalf of the human family is complete. Provisions are made not only for the world as a whole, bringing them back to a state of passive innocence, not only for the sin of Adam, but for the repeated individual transgressions of all sinners. If they will repent of sin and believe the record God gave of his Son, they shall be saved, and saved to the uttermost from all sin and the effects of sin.

Eternity will consummate what time begins, however. What man loses in time, by rejecting proffered grace until manhood or old age, will be to him an eternal loss, though saved at the eleventh hour. He that enters early into the vineyard of the Lord, and bears the burden in the heat of the day, should not question the propriety of the Master of the vineyard standing all the day long in the market-place calling for laborers in his vineyard, offering the last the same as the first; *i. e.*, life, eternal life, since he is the sinner's friend and kinsman, the Redeemer and Saviour of all that will be saved.

Ques. What is the difference between the moral state of the infant world, redeemed by Christ from the curse of the law, without faith, and the moral state of the adult, when justified by faith?

Ans. They are the same, in the sense of passive innocence, the one being redeemed from the effects of sins committed by others, the other justified by faith from the effects of his own transgression, through the imputed merits and righteousness of another. Neither have personal righteousness until they render practical obedience; while the imputed merits of Christ render both, in the eye of justice, passively innocent, and exempt from the curse of the law, Christ having kept the law, and then met the penalty, "That he might be just, and the justifier of him who believeth in Jesus." Keep in mind all goodness is derived from God; evil is also derived from the opposite of good.

In the beginning man's natural moral state was upright and innocent, but not absolutely holy, as God was holy only as far as he rendered practical obedience to the law of love. He was created in God's image, innocent and upright, with capacities to keep the law of love, and thereby derive from the fountain of goodness, through the channels of his faith and obedience, the purity and holiness of the Divine nature, which would transform the soul from passive innocence into the nature of practical godliness or holiness, from grace to grace. For this end was man as a moral agent made upright, that he might keep the law of love, and be a partaker of the Divine nature. For this end was his race redeemed from the effects of sin, and he rendered passively innocent in the view of justice, and again the command was reiterated, "Walk thou before me and be ye perfect," that man might be left without excuse for his unbelief and sin. The provisions of the Gospel are adequate to the wants of man. Jesus Christ, in every sense of the word, is a whole Saviour, and saves to the uttermost all that will come unto him. In another sense, their moral state is alike. Both may be compared to good ground for the reception of good seed; yet if while men sleep, the wicked one sows tares, or in other words, if evil is implanted in the nature of the child by transmission, it will prevent the perfect development of its good nature, the tares will grow out of the ground then as naturally as the wheat, because the neglect to watch to prevent the enemy from sowing tares was sinful. So far the ground becomes stony and hard, bearing thorns, losing its productive nutritious qualities, having no body or depth of earth. This is illustrative of the way-side soil of the human soul once broken up and mellowed by grace, and hardened again by sin.

Ques. What is the difference between the moral state of the justified soul and holiness of heart, without which no man shall see the Lord?

Ans. Justifying faith saves from the penalty of willful transgression, and delivers the captive from prison by paying his debts; but it does not save him from again running into debt and from being again thrown into prison. Yet if he repents and believes even unto seventy times seven, he is each time met by the Good Samaritan, and lifted up, and his debts paid, his wounds dressed and mollified with ointment.

The soul that does not add to his faith virtue, knowledge, temperance, patience, brotherly kindness, and charity, is saved at last, so as by fire, if saved at all. His salvation is like that of the infant world, but his happiness less in degree than that of the infant who was educated in heaven, never having sinned. His vacillating faith will be to him like the devouring flames, to the vast possessions which the child would otherwise lawfully inherit from his father's estate. The flames, though kindled by his own hand, may not cause his father to disown him, yet they will make him *poor in the treasures of the exceeding great rewards,* which can only be distributed by the just, tender Father, among those that love and obey him.

In keeping the commandments there is a great reward. This reward will not be given to the disobedient, or to those saved, so as by fire. The willing and obedient shall eat the good of the land. This practical obedience to the law of love, is holiness. The believer grows up into Christ, his living head, perfecting holiness in the fear of the Lord, by adding to imputed innocence the righteousness of trusting faith. When the righteousness of Christ is imputed to the believing soul, if he abides in this righteousness, he is righteous, even as your Father in heaven is righteous; *i. e.*, he is right, and walking in the right way of life. Therefore it is written, "Be ye holy, for God is holy;" "Be ye perfect, even as your Father which is in heaven is perfect; for he maketh his sun to rise on the evil and the good, and sendeth his rain upon the just and the unjust."

Here is a practical demonstration of the obedience of God to the law of love towards his enemies as well as his children, in doing them all the good he can, even when unsought, whenever and wherever it does not conflict with their moral agency; therefore He says, "Be ye perfect; *i. e.*, in your observance of the law of love, "even as your Father which is in heaven is perfect, and ye shall be the children of your Father which is in heaven." This is the holiness of God. This holiness is goodness, justice, and mercy towards all the works of his hands. "Walk thou before me and be ye perfect," was enjoined by God upon the first Adam, and upon all people in all generations from the beginning of time to the closing scenes of man's earthly probation. "Love is the fulfilling of the law, and love worketh no ill to his neighbor." Show your faith by your works, or your faith is dead, being alone. The soul must have justifying faith to work the works of righteousness. In this sense they must be born again. Unless the faith that once justifies abides in Christ, ye are none of his. The soul must do its first works over again, or "the last state of that man is worse than the first."

"The soul that sinneth, it shall die. The son shall not bear the iniquity of the father, neither shall the father bear the iniquity of the son: the righteousness of the righteous shall be upon him, and the wickedness of the wicked shall be upon him."

"But if the wicked will turn from all his sins that he hath committed, and keep all my statutes, and do that which is lawful and right, he shall surely live, he shall not die."

"All his transgressions that he hath committed, they shall not be mentioned unto him: in his righteousness that he hath done he shall live."

"Have I any pleasure at all that the wicked should die? saith the Lord God, and not that he should return from his ways and live?"

"But when the righteous turneth away from his righteousness, and committeth iniquity, and doeth according to all the abominations that the wicked man doeth, shall he live? All his righteousness that he hath done shall not be mentioned: in his trespass that he hath trespassed, and in his sin that he hath sinned, in them shall he die."

You see that imputed righteousness is the effect of believing faith; so is holiness of heart the effect of practical godliness. Both states are obtained by grace through faith, and only retained by faithful obedience to the law of love. Therefore the Apostle exhorts all believers "to leave the first principles of the doctrine of Christ, and go on to perfection," teaching practical godliness, saying, "Follow peace with all men and holiness, without which no man can see the Lord."

This Scripture is to be understood in the same sense with the precept of Christ, "Blessed are the pure in heart, for they shall see God." To see God and walk with him, the spiritual vision of the believer must be single, eyeing the glory of God in all things; then they see the Lord and he guides them with his eye. "The meek will he guide in judgment, and the meek will he teach his way." The spiritual vision is cleared to behold the Lord in all his works and ways among men, in proportion to his purity, and truly "Blessed are the pure in heart, for they shall see God," and hold converse with him as did Adam, Abraham, and Moses.

He that dwelleth in love, dwelleth in God and God in him. Again, it is written, "Herein is our love made perfect," that we may have boldness in the day of judgment, "because as he is, so are we in this world."

The holiness of the believer is derived from God through obedience and love of the truth. The soul that purely loves God must dwell in love and breathe that atmosphere as his native breath. "There is no fear in perfect love; perfect love casts out fear, because fear hath torment." "He that feareth is not made perfect in love." You see by this last quotation, perfect love, or holiness, implies perfect faith and trust, as well as obedience, the last can not exist without the first; effect follows cause. The believer does not love God with a perfect heart, until he relies with perfect trust and confidence upon his tender care, and believes with a loving heart his every promise, and feels perfect charity towards God, and submission in all the painful and dark dispensation of his permissive providences towards himself, as well as towards others. Let the persecutor destroy and slay him; he must take joyfully the spoiling of his goods, in the hope of a better resurrection to life. When the soul is thus crucified and risen with Christ, he sees the Lord as the text intimates. He knows that his Redeemer lives, and because he lives, he shall live also. He hears the Shepherd's voice, for the Shepherd calls him by name, and leads him out, and he goes before him, and his sheep follow him, and a stranger's voice they will not follow. This is only true of those believers who are born of God in the higher sense of practical godliness, which John refers to bearing the perfect image of Christ's spiritual nature in them. Christ dwelling in them developing their spiritual life. All the impulses of their new resurrection life is in union and harmony with the Divine nature, and opposed to sin and unbelief in every form.

To be thus born of God, and to walk before him in holiness, with a perfect heart and willing mind, is every believers privilege. Such will see the Lord, not as a God that is afar off, as the fearful and unbelieving do, but as a God that is near at hand, ready to help in every time of need, as Job testified when his submission was perfected in suffering; he said, "I have heard of thee by the hearing of the ear, but now mine eye seeth thee."

Again, it is written, "O, taste and see that the Lord is good!" "He that walketh righteously and speaketh uprightly, he that despiseth the gain of oppression, that shaketh his hands from holding bribes, that stoppeth his ears from hearing of blood, and setteth his eyes from seeing evil, he shall dwell on high, his place of defense shall be the munition of rocks, bread shall be given him, his waters shall be sure. His eyes shall see the King in his beauty, they shall behold the land that is very far off. That they may see, and know, and consider, and understand together that the hand of the Lord hath done this."

"Blessed are the pure in heart, for they shall see God." Let your light so shine by practical godliness, that men may see God in your good works, as the pure in heart see God in his works. "Blessed are your eyes for they shall see." "Said I not unto thee, that if thou wouldst believe, thou shouldst see the glory of God?" The contrast is not to be made between the innocent child saved, and the man who walks with God as did Enoch, but between the pure and the impure; and of these, it is written, "Behold, he cometh with clouds, and every eye shall see him, and they that pierced him shall wail because of him. But of the nations that are saved, they shall see his face and his name shall be in their foreheads."

NOTE D.

See Chapter XV., *page* 122.

Ques. If man is not immortal by nature, by what life does he live, not as a Christian, but as a living man?

Ans. We have said organic life was the connecting-link between time and eternity, between spirit and matter, mind and mind, spirit and mind. We now say it is the connecting link between the three worlds before spoken of, as adapted to man's threefold life, (*viz.*,) his physical, intellectual, and spiritual natures, which unity constitutes him a man above the animate creation. His life is a compound of elementary principles employed in the degree required in the creation of all things.

It is not only vitalizing in its life, not only organizing in its nature, not only the propelling and repelling power in matter as manifest in all the elements of nature — not only the vitality of the air, of water, of animal life — but it is when taken as a whole, the vital nature of all created human life, including the intellectual and spiritual, as well as the physical man. Man is endowed, by this upholding organic life, with the power to reproduce his kind. God has promised to add to this created life the eternal life in his Son.

Organic life is embodied in the physical universe of worlds, and operates unseen, imparting intelligence and talent as well as life, to all who live, as mind and spirit in the body operate, upholding all things by its power, in heaven and on earth giving inspiration to genius. This is the upholding power of all created life, whether good or evil, yet this is not the immortality and the eternal life of God promised in his word, with which angel and man were clothed before they sinned, and lost when they sinned, as every sinner though redeemed must lose who violates the law of love.

"He that hateth his brother is a murderer, and ye know that no murderer hath eternal life abiding in him." Man retained his created or natural life after he sinned, but not his spiritual, eternal life, with which he was first clothed, and to which he is now heir too, if obedient. When created life was discociated with immortality and the eternal life of Christ, in whose image man was made, man was no longer a living soul, or an heir of eternal life and immortality, but a mortal dying man. "Dust thou art, and unto dust shalt thou return."

In the day he sinned, he died as heir to eternal life, consequently to eternal happiness. The God of love has made ample provisions for this death in the gift of eternal life in his Son. This gift is unconditional to all the unsinning descendants of Adam, to be given to them at the resurrection of the just, when the mortal shall put on immortality as God's gift. But every where in the Scriptures is eternal life and immortality held forth as conditional to the transgressor, such must seek immortality and eternal life to possess it. It is presented as something which the believer may hope for. This doctrine Jesus taught. "And behold one came unto him and said, good Master, what good thing shall I do that I may have eternal life." Jesus replied, if thou wilt enter into life, keep the commandments, &c. Eternal life is spoken of by Christ, as a state into which the righteous should enter, as a blessing or gift to be inherited. On another occasion a certain lawyer stood up, and tempted him, saying, Master, what shall I do to inherit eternal life? again were the conditions given, "This do and thou shall live." And in connection with this he taught, "He that reapeth receiveth wages and gathereth fruit unto eternal life, that both he that soweth and he that reapeth may rejoice together." Again, a certain young man came to him and asked the same question; the conditions were given, and he went away sorrowful. Do not these instances show that Christ taught this doctrine? it fell upon their unbelieving hearts as new and strange. The pompous Pharisee and unbelieving Jew claimed the Abrahamic succession (as many do now the Apostolic succession), without a Christ in the soul. On other occasions, he said to inquirers, "Search the Scriptures, for in them *ye think ye have eternal life*, and they are they which testify of me;" "And ye will not come unto me that ye might have life." To make this disputed subject still plainer, and put it beyond the question of a doubt, he taught them who had or might have eternal life, "Whoso eateth my flesh and drinketh my blood hath eternal life, and I will raise him up at the last day," (*i. e.*,) bring him to inherit it. The reason given was, "He that eateth my flesh and drinketh my blood dwelleth in me, and I in him." "So he that eateth me shall live by me," otherwise they had no eternal life abiding in them. The subject at issue was life and death, not happiness and misery. The disciples were offended at the doctrine as many will be at this day, "and went back and walked no more with him." Afterwards Jesus said to the twelve, "Will ye also go away." "My sheep hear my voice and they follow me, and I give unto them eternal life, and they shall never perish." We must add, never perish like the goats. Here life and death is contrasted in the most striking language, and the characters who should live and who should perish, and when he shall render judgment to every man according to his deeds. To them who by patient continuence in well doing, seek for glory, and honor, and immortality, and eternal life, shall be given "Glory, honor, and peace, to every man, to the Jew first, and also to the Gentile, for there is no respecter of persons with God," but a respecter of characters.

But unto them that are contentious and do not obey the truth, but obey unrighteousness, "indignation and wrath, tribulation and anguish, upon every soul of man that doeth evil, of the Jew first, and also of the Gentile." Effect follows cause. Obedience brings life, life brings happiness, purity brings peace, disobedience brings sorrow and anguish of spirit, and sorrow worketh death.

If all men by nature were immortal, and possessed eternal life independent of faith in Christ, Christ's teachings were all wrong, for he repeatedly and unequivocally declared he was the only eternal life of the soul, and unless they by faith received him they should "all likewise perish." This doctrine was rejected by the Jewish church; they contended because they had Abraham for their Father, and the oracles of God, they were sure of life and pompously rejected Christ, saying, "Art thou greater than our father Abraham, whom makest thou thyself." Men now contend because Christ has redeemed the world and given them the words of life, placing eternal life and immortality in the future, as the believers strong hope, for which he must seek, "for what a man hath why doth he yet hope for, yet they claim, they are immortal in their sins and have no need of eternal life in Christ, all they want is happiness, and all there is in the denunciations of God against the sinner, resolves back to this, *he shall be unhappy*, notwithstanding God has said, "The soul that sins shall die," that he that speaketh lies shall perish, "Then shall that wicked be revealed whom the Lord shall consume with the spirit of his mouth, and shall destroy with the brightness of his coming," even him whose coming is after the working of Satan, with all power, and signs, and lying wonders, and with all deceivableness of unrighteousness in them that perish, because they receive not the love of the truth that they might be saved. Still they seek not life but happiness, by thus preferring the gifts of God to the giver, they lose both. God does not say, why will ye be miserable? Why will ye not seek true happiness? but "Why will ye die?" for he knows the sinner has a happiness which is not in his service, but in the service of self and sin. The carnal mind finds animal and intellectual happiness in the service of self and the world, neither is the sinner without his happiness, for God sends his rains upon the unjust as well as the just, and makes his sun to rise on the evil as on the good."

They enjoy health and prosperity, and spread themselves like the green bay tree. Their physical beauty, mental endowments, and worldly prosperity, equal if not surpass, the righteous. They have no crosses or self-denials in their life, like the righteous, they put forth the hand of oppression and oppress the poor in the gate, and bind heavy burdens upon the innocent and defenseless, for their own ease and pleasure. The wicked are set upon high places, while the righteous are brought low, and he becomes a by word and filled with reproach, crucified, reviled, and set at naught by the proud defiers of their faith; while they thus oppress virtue, the sinner becomes haughty, heady, highminded, lovers of themselves, more than lovers of God, and say of the Prince of Peace, "There is no beauty in him, that we should desire him." Then how unwise to say happiness was the thing intended instead of life, and misery instead of death, putting cause for effect. Happiness is the result of life as death is the result of sin.

The wicked enjoy equally with the righteous all the pleasures of social life and friendship, all the happiness of domestic relations of home and country, the wealth and the advantages of the arts and sciences which minister abundantly to the necessities, conveniences, and happiness of mankind. God has opened to the sinner as well as to the righteous a wide door for physical and intellectual happiness, and perpetuates and increases them by blessing every effort made in the pursuit of the arts and sciences, to the evil as well as the good. Then in the voice of love and compassion addresses the sinner, not as a miserable or unhappy being, but as a dying soul, pursuing greedily the pleasures and honors of the world in the broad way to death, saying, "Turn ye! turn ye! why will ye die?" "Strait is the gate, and narrow is the way that leads to life, and few there be that find it." Come unto me all ye ends of the earth, and be ye saved, for I am God, and there is none else. Here life is the great pearl held up to the sinner's mind in contrast with death, which is the sinner's final doom. Then it is written, "The devil shall be destroyed and all his works." "The wicked shall be burned up root and branch, then death and hell shall be cast into a lake of fire." "The last enemy that shall be destroyed is death." "Then shall all tears be wiped from every eye, neither shall there be any more sorrow or crying, neither shall there be any more pain, for former things have passed away, and behold I make all things new," and the past shall not come into mind.

God hath said, "The soul that sins shall die." Satan said, thou shalt not surely die. The doctrine is now preached in various ways, (*viz.*,) the perpetuity of the wicked in the second death, making Satan, death, evil, and hell, immortal and eternal as God, and evil infinite. Exalting Satan and his works above all that is called God, saying the soul that has sinned can not die. The second death is perpetuity of being in misery and suffering; God was mistaken, Satan was right, to save the soul from misery (not death,) Jesus became a lamb slain from the foundation of the world, that whosoever believeth on him might be happy as men render it, not saved from the second death, as God declares. He that is often reproved and hardeneth his neck, shall suddenly be miserable, not destroyed, and that without remedy. He that sows to the wind shall reap the whirlwind. The wicked shall be unhappy, not perish, in their own deceivings. Alas! alas! for man's vain reasonings, why will ye die?

The weakness and ignorance of the mind in childhood, idiotcy, and insanity, which is produced from circumstances, with the imbecilities of mind in old age, show that the human mind is by nature changeable, mortal, and dying, as well as the body; both together suffering in sympathy from the loss of the strength, beauty, and symetry, of the vigorous powers with which the first pair were endowed, by the immortality with which Adam was clothed, which brought his newly created powers of body and mind into the vigorous maturity of manhood, and adorned him with godlike beauty, wisdom, and grace, which prepared him at once to hold companionship with God and angels. While thus clothed, his vigorous intellect never wearied; his knowledge and power, like his immortality, were derived from the omnicient and omnipotent God, with whose glory he was clothed. His capacious intellect gave to every beast of the field, and to every creeping and moving thing in the sea, or on the land, and to every bird and fowl of the air, a name, without study or hesitancy, deriving wisdom from the omnicient source.

In his innocent happiness, he began to subdue and possess the garden of the earth, until sin had marked him as his victim, when he was suddenly stripped of all, and became a dying relic of what he once was. He now saw his nakedness, and felt his shame, and the loss of the life, wisdom, glory, and immortality, with which he had been clothed. Begetting in his own likeness, physically, intellectually, and spiritually, his race became like himself, mortal and dying. The effect of sin entailed suffering upon the human family, while death was the penalty for sin.

None of the above changes can be realized by a being possessing inherently by nature, immortality, and eternal life, unless like the Son of God he has power to lay down that life and assume humanity to die, and then to take it again, to redeem by it a lost world. The believer in this world possesses an earnest of his inheritance, his hope of life and immortality entering into that within the vail;

whither Christ his forerunner has gone: "Who hath ascended upon high, led captivity captive, and given gifts to men." These gifts bear the image of his attributes in the saved. A being by nature immortal, can not be corrupted, or increase in wisdom and knowledge, and much less, to change from strength to imbecility, from soundness of mind to insanity, or idiotcy. Yet self-evident facts prove that mind, like the body, can be degraded, corrupted, and decay, because mortal and finite in its nature, until clothed upon with immortality at the resurrection of the just.

Death reigned from Adam to Moses, without the law, as it has since under the law, because sin made man mortal and dying. The Gospel not delivering from physical death, yet making provisions for its redemption, from the power of the grave, and the restoration of the physical powers of soul and body to the Adamic state. "The first Adam was made a living soul, the last Adam a quicken-spirit," the resurrection and the life. At the resurrection morn, and not before, corruption puts on incorruption, and the mortal puts on immortality. For in this we groan earnestly, desiring to be clothed upon with our house which is from heaven. If so be that being clothed, we shall not be found naked, as was Adam. For we that are in this tabernacle, do groan, being burdened; not that we would be unclothed, but clothed upon, that mortality might be swallowed up of life.

Immortality is an attribute of God, and implies perfection and incorruption. God only hath immortality, and dwelleth in the light which no man can approach unto.

The fall of man consists in the loss of the spiritual

image of God in which he was created; the attributes being the lineaments of his moral image. Man can by nature as justly lay claim to omniscience and omnipresence, as he can to the immortality of God, yet his senses guide his judgment in this particular, and not his creed. Do men reason man is immortal by nature, because mind is capacitated to think, perceive, reflect, compare, and judge, above the brute creation?

The capabilities of the mortal man, even which are but the dying relics of what he was when he came from the hands of his Maker, are but in part appreciated by the wise. His abilities do far, yea, very far, exceed the powers now ascribed by man to immortal beings. Blessed, yea blessed, are they that shall have a part in the first resurrection. They which have borne the image of the earthly, shall then bare the image of the heavenly. When men wake up at the resurrection morn and feel the change the permeating, vitalizing, and revivifying power which eternal life will give to the soul and body united, covered with immortal glory by the balmy breath of all God's attributes, as at first when restored to the meridian strength of the matured powers of manhood; while the soul quickening atmosphere of heaven shall send the life current of immortality coursing through his veins, qualifying him to grasp the new unfolding mysteries of the omniscient mind, which is equally his privilege to enjoy with immortality, then add to this all the other qualities of the divine mind in whose image man was first made, then he will begin to appreciate the nature of the redemption wrought out by Christ for man, then he will realize the vast difference between the capacities of a mortal dying man and of being raised to newness of life, clothed with immortality, of which he is destitute while living in the body or out of the body, until the resurrection morn, for the believer in Christ is saved by hope; for what a man hath why doth he yet hope for.

This hope of eternal life brings a present Christ into the soul, and he now begins to live that life by faith in the Spirit which he is heir to, and will enter into the possessions of, at that glorious resurrection morn. These are some of the gifts given to men who receive and obey the law of Love, and seek for glory, immortality, and eternal life, from him who only hath it to give who is the only potentate, the Lord of Lords, and King of Kings.

The senses of the spiritual body will aid the perceptions there, as the senses of the mortal body do, the perceptions here.

Do you ask how and in what degree, the redeemed soul will participate even in the resurrection state, in the gifts alluded to, of the omniscience, and omnipresence, and omnipotence of God, in whose image they were created?

We reply in the degree in which he seeks it, then, as now. The finite capacities of the mortal mind, will there bear the image of the infinite, capacitated to range through infinite space, with the speed of thought to understand and know the will and purposes of the Creator in all his work, as mind explores mind and thought perceives thought, from the babe in Christ to the highest seraphim of light, and onward to the throne of the Deity, through the divinity of the attributes aided by the Holy Spirit of Truth, until these attributes so pervade and permeate the soul, that it shall reflect the image of the heavenly. Then shall ye be like him, for ye shall see him as he is, and be changed into his image, from glory to glory.

This glorified state succeeds the millenial and the last judgement day. Then shall the deserted plains of heaven's realm once vocal with songs of angelic hosts, resound the praise of God and the Lamb. The ransomed of the Lord possessing their vacated thrones and dominions, bearing their palms and crowns, and casting them in the seraphic blaze of adoring worship at Jesus' feet.

This is a faint representation of the life purchased for man, and reserved unto the judgment of the great day, for its perfect consummation. The resurrection life is preparatory to the millenial state, the millenial to the glorified state, which succeeds the judgment.

Wisdom and knowledge is graduated in level plains, from the foundations of the deep, to the throne of the eternal. "I wisdom dwell with prudence and find out knowledge of witty invention."

" When he laid the foundations of the deep I was with him."

"He that made the earth by his power, he hath established the world by his wisdom, and hath stretched out the heavens by his discretion."

You see from the last quotation, power, wisdom, and discretion, were all employed in this work of creation, yet they are not one and the same thing. Neither is the life which is employed in the creation of man or worlds, in the sense of its continuance the same as the eternal life, which alone perpetuates the existance of man or angel. Let minds make this distinction, they will understand why the soul that sins can die as well the body, and why a lively hope in Christ is necessary to perpetuate eternal life in dying men. While he whose is the wisdom, and the power, and the discretion, hath said, in the day that thou eatest thereof, thou shalt surely die. Again he hath said, the heavens and the earth shall pass away, and the powers of the heavens shall be shaken, but my words shall not pass away.

Here let your anxious mind rest, the builder is greater than the house. The works of God are not necessarily eternal in their duration of existance, because created by the eternal God, especially if that finite existance is conditional upon obedience, and the soul disobeys.

NOTE E.

See close of Chapter XIX., *page* 167.

THE day of retribution will come to the destroyer of God's heritage. He will there be held by the divine power of the Son of God. Humbled and brought low before his own destroyed subjects, by the power he has defied, to receive back suffering in kind and degree, which his wiles had inflicted upon others. His power of endurance continually filled to the extreme of agony, until the sentence is executed, when "Satan shall be destroyed and all his works."

As ages on ages roll away, as generation has succeeded generation, will the action of nature's laws perpetuate in the minds of each and all, the part they have acted in life's great drama by portraying the same scenes, as they were enacted, and as they were recorded in space, and rolled together as a scroll, and cast into the burning pit, while the elements shall melt with fervent heat, and reveal in liquid flames, in the outer darkness, and in the lake of fire and brimstone, each murderous scene of hate, of envy, of lust, of vice, and crime of every sort and kind, committed by apostate angel or man. Each suffering according to deeds done, until the penalty of death is executed, reaping just what they have sown.

For these have no Saviour to mitigate their woes, or cover with his pierced hand their crimson sins. Him they despised, set at naught, and rejected, saying, let our sins fall upon us, and on our children. These turned a deaf ear to love and mercy, and were given up to their own chosen way, and to the power of the second death.

The worm that never dies is no part of the soul, but figurative of the executioner's work, which feeds upon it, while there is consciousness to prey upon. Jesus taught, "If thy hand offend thee, cut it off and cast it from thee, for it is better for thee to enter into life maimed, than having two hands to go into hell, into the fire that never shall be quenched; where the worm dieth not, and the fire is not quenched."

The fire which can never be quenched, is the consuming fire of God's love, held beforé the guilty conscience of both angel and man. God, out of Christ, is a consuming fire to the sinner; these have not Christ. There every knee shall bow, and every tongue confess the justice of their doom instead of blaspheming his name, yet there is no remedy. Death is the penalty for sin; Satan is first destroyed, then all his works; this is the second death. Yea, blessed are they that have a part in the first resurrection, over such the second death hath no power; to such he will say, "Well done good and faithful servant, enter thou into the joy of thy Lord." "Eye hath not seen, nor ear heard, neither hath it entered into the heart of man, to conceive of the glory which he hath prepared for them that love him," and who have followed him in the regeneration. Then with glorified bodies which will outshine the sun in its strength, with enlarged intellects, equal to grasp the wondrous unfolding mysteries of infinite wisdom, led on by the Holy Spirit of Truth throughout the ceaseless ages of eternity, will man go forth to explore the heights, and depths, and lengths, and breadths, of love divine. Admitted (as were the angels who kept not their first estate), to the presence chamber of the King of Kings, and Lord of Lords, to behold the glory of the infinite perfections of the Deity, as their capacities are prepared to contemplate and participate in the glories of immortality and eternal life, being made heirs of God and joint heirs with Christ.

Now call to mind what Jesus said. How full of meaning are those precious words, "Father, I will that they also whom thou hast given me, be with me where I am, that they may behold my glory, which thou hast given me, which I had with thee before the world was, for these have believed thou didst send me. That they may be one in me, as I, Father, art in thee, and thou in me, that they may be one in us." This includes the highest glory which Christ, as a Son, had with the Father.

The glory which the aspiring angels claimed as their own, and claiming, without accepting it, through the divinely appointed means, the well beloved Son, they fell, and lost their inheritance to life as well as bliss, which fallen man, seeking by faith, obtains.

Glory, honor, praise, and power,
Unto the Lamb be given,
Whom, by His own heart's blood,
Redeemed man from sin and death,
And from the oppressions of the Devil healed
That he might live.
Glory to the Lamb that was slain,
Let thrones, and dominions, and powers, proclaim,
While cherubim and seraphim join
In the songs of the redeemed;
When crowns and robes of victory are given
By the Lamb, to the saints who have overcome
The world, the flesh, and sin.

The divine unity in the Father, Son, and Holy Spirit, became the test of angelic allegiance and obedience, as the tree of knowledge became the test of man's obedience. Neither were designed to be such by God, but were made so by the transgressor. "God can not be tempted with evil, neither tempteth he any man." Obedience was both easy and natural, as well as suitable and comely to each, (*i. e.*,) angel and Adam. The time had arrived which made this development of truth necessary, for the increased knowledge and felicity of the heavenly hosts, as well as to the race of man. Angelic minds are well qualified and prepared through the teachings of the Holy Spirit, to render the homage and worship, demanded of the angels by the Father, to be given to the Son.

So was the first pair qualified to resist evil as well as well as obey. Had they obeyed in implicit faith, all would have been well, unless another transgressor had arisen. Yet free to act, as all created intelligent minds must be, who derive their life, knowledge, and happiness, from their Creator, and are rewarded for their willing obedience to the law of Love, these commands and prohibitions were necessary, to secure their happiness and well being.

The doctrine of the trinity in unity, was the glory of the angels, as well as of man. Before they fell the Son of God was given to inspire their angelic devotions, and enhanced their joy and elevation by his gifts, which are beyond comparison.

The shadow of the reality is portrayed by the pen of inspiration, in the record of the second death. This only shows what they lost, but not what they would have gained by their faith and steadfastness, and worship of the Son.

Hence, how befitting the Father of "love" should say, "this is my beloved Son, let all the angels of God worship him."

Fathom, if you can, the wonder and silence of angels, as they began to appreciate the benefit of the presence, and gift of the Son of God to the worshiping hosts of heaven, when they learned the stipulations that were made between the Father and the Son, for the redemption of man. All heaven beheld with astonishment his love when he lay down his life and glory for man, and become as a Lamb slain from the foundation of the world, (*i. e.*,) from the period of Adam's transgression.

Man in paradise, as well as angels in heaven, were taught great truths by figures or symbols. John the revelator in vision, saw in the New Jerusalem, "the tree of life on either side of the river, and the leaves of the trees were for the healing of the nations," (or the health of the nations). This tree was emblematic of Christ the eternal life.

The tree of life in the garden had the same signification on earth as in heaven, to portray to man that Christ the Son of God, in whose image he was made, was the only eternal life of the soul. Of that tree, man might eat and live for ever. To teach him that his life was derived from a self-existent source, and to live, he must continue to receive it day by day, that when he disobeyed the law of life he must die. Christ asserted, "Except ye eat my flesh and drink my blood, ye have no life in you."

The tree of knowledge portrayed that satanic spirits were abroad to induce them to seek knowledge from forbidden sources, whom they must resist. Being capacitated to receive good from spiritual agencies, by the same law of mind, moral agency could listen to evil. Therefore God said, "Of the tree of knowledge of good and evil thou shalt not eat." "In the day thou eatest thereof, thou shalt surely die." They understood its deep signification, hence neither the woman or the man expressed any surprise at the appearance of such a foe as Satan, but the woman simply replied in the vindication of herself, "The serpent beguiled me," deceived me, and "I did eat." She knew his history; their's was not the sin of ignorance, hence their fall. Learn from this, God never tempts man with evil, but warns him of evil, and forbids evil, to save his life and secure his happiness. He tries man's faith by requiring him to forego a present seeming good, to obtain a greater future good, to discipline his affections and chasten his curiosity, and subdue his will, that in his ignorance of the future, he may trustingly believe God as did Abraham, and walk by naked faith, thereby add to their gifts the graces of the spirit. This work of bearing the daily cross tests their faith, their trust, their endurance, their fidelity to the cause of truth, before they begin to reap the good promised. Temptations to evil and unbelief in God, comes from Satan, while the trial of your faith comes from God, because knowledge is limited. Then he rewards the confidence and trust of the faithful soul with robes and crowns of light.

Think not Jesus the beloved of the Father is all your own. O, earth! worlds on worlds adore him, for whom he obtains of the Father, dominion and glory unutterable.

This, Paul saw, when caught up to heaven, which enabled him to count all things but loss, for the excellency of the knowledge of Christ Jesus our Lord. This knowledge of the glory and happiness, which he saw the crucified had transfused through countless worlds as well as earth, made earthly pomp appear like dross to the glory of the cross of Christ.

Think you the heavenly host beheld with indifferent gaze the scenes of Bethlehem? The suffering from the manger to the cross?

Think you, their astonishment is lessened at the half heartedness of his followers; at their great indifference to spiritual things, to gain honor among men, and gold to shine?

Hear, O heavens! and give ear, O earth! They leave their own souls and their fellow man, to perish in the flames of the second death, to acquire the honor, fame, and wealth of a day, which is to end with time.

O! haste thee on thy mission!
Proclaim this truth to man:
Before thrice seven times eleven moons

Shall fill their round,
This earth by waring armies will be spanned.
The armies of Gog and Magog,
To battle will array;
The doctrines of Popery,
With leaders dark and bold,
The doctrines of Antichrist,
These new lights unfold;
The dragon and the beast,
To make one proselyte,
Will compass sea and land,
These armies to unite.
O! haste thee on thy mission!
These wonders, let the pen proclaim;
Fear not their non-fulfillment,
Thy God will thee sustain,
Thy work is crucifying,
Yet near and distant
This message must be given,
To other lands and people,
To other climes and realms;
Before kings and princes,
Before tribunals let it stand;
The voice of truth shall break
The fetters of the land.
The soul that seeks salvation,
From self, death, and sin,
The soul that asks direction,
Will sure protection find,
And wage successful war,
Against the man of sin.
Then haste thee on thy mission!
Thou trembling worm
Fear not the face of clay, of woman born,
His day is fast departing;
His glory and renown
Is like the meteor's blaze,
That first dazzles, then falls,
With a lurid flame.
Still haste thee on thy mission!
To man let the words of truth be given;
To all who will listen, by
The reapers will be gathered in
To the marriage supper of the Lamb.

Will not this repay thee,
For all thy toil and care,
For all thou may'st suffer,
The message to prepare?
To behold the ransomed thousands,
As they bow before the throne,
Who were startled from their dreamy sleep,
By this warning echo from the throne?

www.ingramcontent.com/pod-product-compliance
Lightning Source LLC
LaVergne TN
LVHW010244110826
845151LV00004B/1383

* 9 7 8 1 4 2 5 5 2 3 2 9 9 *